SERIAL KILLERS

Ted Bundy

The Campus Killer

by Rebecca Morris

Essential Library
An Imprint of Abdo Publishing
abdobooks.com

ABDOBOOKS.COM

Published by Abdo Publishing, a division of ABDO, PO Box 398166, Minneapolis, Minnesota 55439.

Printed in China.
102024
012025

THIS BOOK CONTAINS RECYCLED MATERIALS

Cover Photo: Bill Waterson/Alamy
Interior Photos: Mark Levy/AP Images, 4–5; Carol M. Highsmith/Buyenlarge/Archive Photos/Getty Images, 7; David Williams/Bloomberg/Getty Images, 9; Aspen Historical Society, Aspen Times Collection, 11, 22; Russ Carmack/The News Tribune/AP Images, 15–16; Pictures Now/Alamy, 20; Andrey Popov/iStockphoto, 24–25; G. E. Kidder Smith/Corbis Historical/VCG/Getty Images, 28; Shutterstock Images, 31; Olivier Douliery/ABACAUSA.com/Newscom, 34; Spring Images/Alamy, 36–37; Salt Lake City Deseret News/AP Images, 39; AP Images, 42, 69, 83, 84; Education Images/Universal Images Group/Getty Images, 46; Gary Stewart/AP Images, 48–49; Bettmann/Getty Images, 50, 70, 80–81, 90–91; Virrage Images/Shutterstock Images, 53; Hulton Archive/Getty Images, 54; GL Archive/Alamy, 57; Ken Hawkins/Alamy, 60, 85; Ross Dolan/Glenwood Springs Post-Independent/AP Images, 62–63, 64; FBI, 72–73; Acey Harper/The Chronicle Collection/Getty Images, 74; Phil Sandlin/AP Images, 92; Brian Douglas/Netflix/GDA/AP Images, 98

Editor: Marley Richmond
Series Designer: Joshua Olson

Library of Congress Control Number: 2024938312

PUBLISHER'S CATALOGING-IN-PUBLICATION DATA

Names: Morris, Rebecca, author.
Title: Ted Bundy: the campus killer / by Rebecca Morris
Other title: the campus killer
Description: Minneapolis, Minnesota: ABDO Publishing, 2025 | Series: Serial killers | Includes online resources and index.
Identifiers: ISBN 9781098295387 (lib. bdg.) | ISBN 9798384916383 (ebook)
Subjects: LCSH: Bundy, Ted--Juvenile literature. | Killers (Murderers)--Biographies --Juvenile literature. | Serial killers--Biographies--Juvenile literature. | Crime--Juvenile literature. | True crime stories--Juvenile literature.
Classification: DDC 364.15232--dc23

CONTENTS

This book discusses accounts of crime, violence, and death that may be disturbing to some readers.

CHAPTER 1

JAILBREAK IN COLORADO

On the morning of June 7, 1977, Judge George Lohr slammed down his gavel, calling for a recess at Pitkin County Courthouse in Aspen, Colorado. Proceedings halted on pretrial motions the court was hearing for a murder charge. Ted Bundy rose and walked into the law library. No one thought much of Bundy walking freely through the courtroom, despite the fact that Bundy himself was the accused murderer.

Perhaps due to Bundy's well-known charm, or because his presence in the law library had become routine, Bundy's guards had become lenient. That summer day

Ted Bundy wore many layers of clothing when he walked into Pitkin County Courthouse on June 7, 1977. He had on pants, two pairs of shorts, four shirts, and a sweater.

PREPARING TO ESCAPE

Bundy waited for the snow to melt in Colorado while he prepared for his escape. In March, Judge Lohr had granted Bundy's request to represent himself in court. Although Bundy was not experienced in the legal field, he had attended some law school. Bundy's presence in the law library was an accepted part of courtroom proceedings. In addition, Bundy's attorney had successfully petitioned for him to appear in court without shackles. The week before his planned escape, Bundy had cut his hair and shaved his face, hoping he would be unrecognizable from the most recent photos of himself. His preparations proved helpful to his escape.

was warm. The windows in the second-story library were left open.

When a guard stepped into the hallway for a break, Bundy casually walked toward the window. Then, when no one was looking, he jumped out. "I can still feel the jolt of hitting the ground," Bundy later recalled.[1]

He landed outside the courthouse, unnoticed by passersby, and began to run. Blocks from the building, Bundy stopped to strip off the extra layers of clothing he wore in preparation for his escape. Soon he was in the foothills of Aspen Mountain, while more than 100 searchers began to comb the city and mountain trails looking for him.[2]

A Breaking Point

Bundy was already a known criminal when he was charged with murder in October 1976. On March 1 of that year, he had been convicted of kidnapping 18-year-old Carol DaRonch in Utah. While Bundy was serving his sentence in Utah, Colorado police uncovered evidence connecting him to the murder of Caryn Campbell, a 23-year-old who had gone missing from an Aspen ski lodge on January 12, 1975. Bundy was extradited to Colorado for the trial. He had begun planning his escape immediately after learning about the charge.

Into the Night

In a stroke of luck for Bundy, the search parties headed north while he began his trek south. Bundy's plan was to

It took approximately ten minutes for anyone inside Pitkin County Courthouse to realize Bundy had escaped.

head toward Crested Butte, a city separated from Aspen by tall mountains. He would then make his way toward the East Coast, where he hoped to find anonymity.

Bundy was hopeful as he began his climb. "I was faintly amused, too, because I knew they didn't know where I was," he recalled.[3] But his good humor started to fade as the sun set and the evening turned cold. Soon it was pitch black and raining. Bundy's legs began to give out from exhaustion. He had climbed straight up a mountain for hours without stopping, gaining more than 3,000 feet (900 m) of elevation.[4]

"He said it was just too nice a day to stay inside."[5]

—Sergeant Don Davis, recalling Bundy's reason for running

Although Bundy was afraid to stop moving, he knew he needed to rest. His pace had slowed until he could barely cover half a mile (0.8 km) each hour. He decided to backtrack to an abandoned cabin he had seen earlier. He arrived there at approximately 4:00 a.m. on June 8.

Inside the cabin, Bundy ate what food he could find and slept for several hours. He grabbed a flashlight and coat to prepare himself for the conditions outside. Once the sun set, Bundy left his warm refuge and continued toward Crested Butte.

On the proper trails, a hiker could cross the mountains surrounding Aspen and reach Crested Butte after walking approximately ten miles (16 km).

Wrong Turns

Bundy hiked through the night and into the growing daylight of the following morning. While he had been in the cabin, search parties had gotten closer. He saw smoke from their campsites on the mountain below him and knew he needed to adjust his course.

Bundy had no map or knowledge of the mountains around Aspen. He decided to take an animal trail up the mountainside, hoping to skirt around the searchers below. Bundy followed dangerous, grueling paths for many hours. By the evening of June 10, he reached the top of the trail he had climbed. With a better vantage point,

SEARCH PARTIES

Once Bundy's escape was discovered, both law enforcement personnel and regular citizens joined search parties. Police set up roadblocks around Aspen, hoping to catch Bundy if he left the city by car. Specially trained dogs were brought in to track Bundy's scent. The dogs were presented with Bundy's sweater to find his scent, but they instead picked up that of the officer who had brought the sweater. Bad weather thwarted later efforts to use tracking dogs. When the search was unsuccessful by its second day, the Federal Bureau of Investigation (FBI) joined the hunt.

Bundy realized he had traveled in the wrong direction. He could see Aspen in the distance, not Crested Butte. He later said, "I knew I'd made a serious, *serious* error."[6]

Above the tree line, Bundy was in danger of being seen. He quickly reversed course. Bundy injured his legs in his rush to make it down the mountain. By the morning of June 11, he had gone days without sleep and couldn't find water. He could barely walk and was confused from exhaustion. Out of desperation, he decided to return to the cabin.

When he reached his former refuge, Bundy saw hundreds of footprints surrounding the building. His previous break-in had been discovered. "It would be hard for me to describe the sheer and utter panic I felt when I saw those prints," he said.[7]

While he stood outside the cabin, Bundy heard helicopters flying overhead. He believed he would be discovered at any moment. He rethought his plan, deciding to head back to Aspen and steal a car.

An Unexpected Catch

Bundy retreated from the cabin, but he didn't make it far before a man caught sight of him. Pointing his gun at Bundy's head, the man let Bundy know that he wasn't welcome on his private property. He said there was a manhunt going on. He was clearly suspicious of Bundy. However, it didn't seem as though he recognized Bundy.

Sheriff deputies stood outside the cabin where Bundy had previously rested and found food.

Bundy quickly turned on his charm. He claimed to know nothing about the man they were searching for. Instead, Bundy claimed to be a dentist with a wife and children. The man reluctantly believed this story. Bundy walked away slowly. He stopped periodically to pick flowers, hoping he would appear less suspicious, as if he wasn't in a hurry to escape.

UNHEEDED WARNINGS

Once Bundy made up his mind to escape, he needed a plan. But he knew nothing about how to escape. He started by talking to other inmates who had attempted their own flights for freedom. Some of these inmates informed the guards about Bundy's plans. Officials also read several of Bundy's letters to friends that hinted at his upcoming getaway. Officers increased Bundy's security behind bars, but their added vigilance did not extend to the courtroom where his pretrial hearing was being held. Instead of scrapping his plan, Bundy simply changed his exit point from jail to the courthouse.

Bundy's luck held when he reached Aspen. The fourth car he tried was left open with keys underneath the driver's seat.

But his luck wouldn't last long. At approximately 2:00 a.m. on June 13, two officers saw Bundy swerving on the road. They turned on their lights, signaling that Bundy should pull over. The officers believed the driver to be drunk.

One of the officers in the squad car had worked at the jail where Bundy had been held. Bundy thought, "Now this is Gene Flatt, who for 70 days as a Pitkin County deputy served me breakfast every morning."[8] At first, Flatt didn't identify Bundy. But when Bundy was unable to produce a driver's license, Flatt began to recognize the man in front of him. The two officers called in backup, and Bundy's identity was confirmed.

After being on the run for six days, covering about 50 miles (80 km) of wilderness, and losing 30 pounds (14 kg), Bundy's run was over.[9] Police took him back to the Garfield County Jail. There, Bundy would continue to await the murder trial he could not escape.

CHAPTER 2

BUILDING A FACADE

Theodore "Ted" Robert Cowell was born on November 24, 1946, in Burlington, Vermont. His mother, Eleanor Louise Cowell, was 22 years old and unmarried. At the time, society held stigmas about single mothers. Cowell gave birth to Ted at the Elizabeth Lund Home for Unwed Mothers. Single mothers could receive support at homes such as this one. Rumors at the time said Ted's father was a sailor named Jack Worthington. Although Eleanor likely knew who the man was, his identity has never been official public knowledge.

East Coast to West Coast

Cowell moved back to her parents' home in Philadelphia, Pennsylvania, after Ted was born. Ted spent the first few years of his life there with his grandparents, mother, and aunts. In 1951, Cowell and Ted moved across the country to the Tacoma, Washington, area. Shortly before the move,

Ted's mother spoke to him on the phone from the family's home in Tacoma, Washington. She lived there until her death in 2012.

Cowell changed Ted's last name to Nelson. She believed it would help to protect him from any embarrassment he might face for having a single mother.

While Ted's mother looked for a job in Washington, she and Ted lived with Jack Cowell, Ted's great-uncle. Soon, Ted's mother got a job as a secretary. In May 1951, just a few months after the move to Washington, she married John Culpepper Bundy, or Johnnie to those who knew him. Bundy was a US Navy veteran who Eleanor met at a church social event. Bundy adopted Ted, and Ted took his last name.

Eleanor and Johnnie had four more children together: two daughters, Linda and Sandra, born in 1952 and 1956, and two sons, Glenn and Richard, born in 1954 and 1961. The family lived in a few different houses before purchasing a home near Puget Sound in Tacoma when Ted was in elementary school. Ted lived there for the rest of his childhood.

TED'S FATHER

It is uncertain how Ted learned that his father's identity was unknown. One person close to Ted recalled that he found out from his cousin John. According to this account, John showed Ted his birth certificate during a childhood argument. The word *unknown* appeared on the certificate in the place marked for his father's name. Ted was humiliated. Ted himself claimed he found the birth certificate when he was in high school. His childhood friend Terry Storwick observed that Ted felt upset and abandoned.

Putting on a Mask

Certain events in Ted's early life confused and angered the boy, including his father's abandonment, his family's move from Philadelphia to Washington, and his mother's marriage. Ted later said he loved Johnnie, but they had a complicated relationship. Even as a child, Ted viewed Johnnie as uneducated and was critical of him for it. Ted often argued with Johnnie.

In one of these arguments, Ted's close friend Terry Storwick saw Johnnie swing his arm at Ted as if he were going to hit the boy. Storwick later said in an interview, "It wasn't that Johnnie was an unreasonable man; I think his temper was a reaction to Ted's animosity."[1]

Ted struggled with disappointments and insecurities during his childhood and teenage years. He was bitter about his biological father's abandonment of their family. Ted also felt self-conscious about his family's middle-class income and embarrassed by their modest material possessions.

At school, Ted lost an election to be vice president of the student council, and he did not earn a place on the basketball or baseball teams he wanted to be on. He later said these disappointments made him feel lost and left out. He often felt a lack of confidence or like he did not know how to fit in with his peers. "I didn't know what underlay social interactions," Ted said.[2]

Ted began to compartmentalize his life. He developed a mask that hid his suffering, loneliness, and embarrassment. Ted focused on his outward appearance. At school, he presented himself well in class. He dressed nicely and used good manners. His classmates considered him likable, charming, good-looking, and well-spoken.

"In my early schooling, it seemed like there was no problem in learning what the appropriate social behaviors were. It just seemed like I hit a wall in high school."[4]

–Ted Bundy, describing his social struggles in high school

Ted's mask seemed to work, even if he himself didn't believe it.

Behind this facade, Ted tried to hide certain concerning behaviors. One of these behaviors was abusing animals. Ted purchased mice from a pet store and brought them to the woods. There, he would release some of the mice but kill and dismember others. He also developed a lifelong habit of stealing things he wanted or needed.

College Years

In 1965, Bundy graduated from Wilson High School. That fall, he began college at the University of Puget Sound, where he had gotten a scholarship. After a year, he transferred to the University of Washington in Seattle.

Bundy met Diane Edwards at the University of Washington in the spring of 1967. She became his first serious girlfriend. Edwards was from a wealthy family in San Francisco, California. She had many qualities Bundy admired. Bundy described Edwards as "a beautiful dresser, beautiful girl. Very personable. Nice car, great parents."[3]

In 1967, Bundy received a scholarship to a summer program at Stanford University's Chinese Institute. Attending would allow him to advance his studies and be in California near Edwards for the summer. However, Bundy struggled with the coursework and had a hard time fitting in among the other students.

That fall, Edwards broke up with Bundy. She viewed Bundy as immature and believed he did not have a clear direction for his academics or his future. After the breakup, Bundy's brother Glenn said, "He came home and seemed pretty upset and moody. I'd never seen him like that before."[5] Bundy also described his relationship with Edwards as something that "had a lasting impact on me."[6]

SHOPLIFTING

Ted used theft as a way to get the expensive items he wanted but could not afford. Before entering a store to shoplift, Ted put on a nice suit so he would look unassuming and forgettable. He also drank alcohol to calm his nerves. "I didn't want to be looking over my shoulder and appear nervous," Ted said.[7] Sometimes the things he stole were unimportant. Ted once walked out of a greenhouse holding a tree that was eight feet (2.4 m) tall, for which he had not paid. Although Ted continued stealing throughout his life, he was never caught as a shoplifter.

Still upset about the end of his relationship with Edwards, Bundy did not go back to the University of Washington for his next semester in 1968. Instead,

During his first years of college, Bundy focused his studies on Asian history and language. He dreamed of working for the State Department as an ambassador to China.

he spent time traveling. In the summer of 1969, he settled back in Washington. He rented a room in an older couple's house in the University District of Seattle. Bundy helped them with maintenance at the house, and the couple liked him. He would live there for the next five years.

A New Start

In the fall of 1969, Bundy met Elizabeth Kendall at a bar. Kendall had just moved to the area from Utah. She was divorced and had a young daughter. Kendall found Bundy charming and attractive, and the two began a relationship.

Soon after meeting Kendall, Bundy returned to the University of Washington. He graduated in 1972 with high grades and a bachelor's degree in psychology.

Bundy began working as a counselor at a mental health clinic. He held that job for only a short time. One report from Bundy's time as a counselor stated that he was "not capable of being emotionally responsive to the needs of his clients and patients."[8]

Eventually Bundy left his counseling job. He began to work for political campaigns. He also applied for law school, but his applications were all rejected.

During this time, Bundy's mask was still in place. In secret, he continued to practice abusive behaviors. He peeped into women's windows at night. He continued his habit of stealing. He also lied to Kendall often and began to date other women. In July 1973, Bundy flew to San Francisco to

A CHAMELEON

Experts have compared Bundy to a chameleon because of his ability to change his appearance and adopt false identities. Bundy realized that small changes, such as using a fake mustache, growing a beard, or styling his hair in a new way, made a significant impact on his appearance. He used his skill to change and hide his identity in his political work. While working on Governor Daniel Evans's re-election campaign, Bundy gathered information about the governor's opponent by pretending to be a graduate student conducting research for a paper.

Kendall, *right*, said she saw Bundy, *left*, as someone she might marry.

meet his ex-girlfriend, Diane Edwards. Bundy and Edwards rekindled their romance. For the coming months, Bundy would secretly date both women.

Continued Lies

Bundy's second round of law school applications proved successful and earned him admission to the University of Utah, to begin in the fall of 1973. Soon after, an acquaintance convinced Bundy that the University of Puget Sound would be a better institution for Bundy's legal education. Bundy applied to Puget Sound and was accepted. He withdrew from Utah.

However, Bundy quickly began to struggle with the coursework at Puget Sound. He saw the school and the other students as beneath him, and this became Bundy's excuse for the poor effort he applied to his studies. Once again, Bundy changed his mind. He reapplied to the University of Utah and was accepted.

Bundy's failures caused him inner turmoil, and his respectable outer facade continued to hide a darker version of himself. Edwards came to visit Bundy during his winter break, and she left believing they were engaged. Kendall, too, was still happily in love with Bundy. But the peace wouldn't last much longer.

CHAPTER 3

DISAPPEARANCES IN THE NORTHWEST

Karen Sparks, an 18-year-old student at the University of Washington, was in her bedroom reading at 1:00 a.m. on January 4, 1974. Sparks's bedroom was in a home she shared with three friends in the University District of Seattle. Even though the room was on the basement level, there was an outside window that looked into the room. As Sparks was reading, something at the window caught her eye. There seemed to be a man watching her.

Sparks had also seen a man looking at her while she was at a laundromat close to her home days before. Sparks did not worry over that incident. She dismissed the man at her window on January 4 as well. She thought it might simply be her imagination playing tricks on her. She soon went to sleep for the night.

At 2:00 a.m., the man from the window crept into Sparks's bedroom and attacked her. He beat her with a

Sparks said the incident on January 4 was not the first time she had seen a man watching her. However, it was the first time the man had broken in.

metal object until she was unconscious. He also sexually assaulted her with another object. Sparks's roommates found her much later that day, after 7:00 p.m., and called for help.

Sparks did not regain consciousness for more than a week. The assault caused severe internal injuries. It also damaged her vision and hearing. She could not give police information about the man who assaulted her because she was unable to remember the attack. Only Bundy, her attacker, knew the full details of what happened that night.

Gone in the Night

Less than a month later, Bundy broke into another University of Washington student's bedroom. The bedroom belonged to 21-year-old Lynda Ann Healy. Healy was well-known in the community for doing the ski report on a local morning radio program.

She had spent the night of January 31 with her roommates. The group got home late. Around midnight, Healy went to her bedroom.

At 5:30 a.m. on February 1, one of Healy's roommates woke to the sound of Healy's alarm clock going off. The roommate went to Healy's room and found it empty, which was unusual. However, there were no signs of violence. Nothing was out of place, except that Healy's bed was made, which was not typical for her.

Not long after that, the radio station called to ask where Healy was. She had not arrived to do the ski report. When no one saw Healy for the rest of the day,

INTERRUPTED ATTACK

When Sparks spoke about her attack years later, she said she believed Bundy intended to kill her. However, Sparks suspected a noise interrupted the attack. One of Sparks's roommates slept in a nearby bedroom and had a habit of talking in his sleep. Sparks believed the sound of a man speaking close by frightened Bundy into stopping the attack and leaving the scene.

her roommates and family grew concerned, and her mother called police.

The responding officers observed that Healy's room was neat and orderly with no immediate sign of a crime. However, when police pulled away the bedspread, they found bloodstains on one of the pillows and the sheets around it. The pillowcase was also missing from the pillow. In the closet, police found Healy's nightgown hanging up. The nightgown had a bloodstain around the back of the neck area.

The only other things missing in the room were Healy's backpack and one outfit. There was little evidence of a crime, so police initially believed Healy had gotten a nosebleed and went for help. However, that theory did not explain why Healy had disappeared without speaking to anyone, including her roommates, boyfriend, parents, or employers. Police talked to more than 65 people about Healy's disappearance, but they found little information that could solve the case.[1]

Five More Disappearances

While police searched for information about Healy's disappearance, Bundy continued to abduct women for the next several months. In these abductions,

Manson disappeared from Evergreen State College, approximately 70 miles (113 km) southwest of the University of Washington.

Bundy changed his pattern and took women from public places rather than attacking them in their bedrooms. All the disappearances occurred at night or in the dark, early morning hours.

Donna Gail Manson was the next to disappear after Healy. She vanished the night of March 12 after leaving her dorm. On April 17, Susan Elaine Rancourt, an 18-year-old student at Central Washington State College, disappeared at about 10:00 p.m. after leaving a meeting on campus.

In May, Bundy drove 260 miles (418 km) to Corvallis, Oregon, to commit his next abduction. Roberta Kathleen Parks disappeared after leaving her dorm room on May 6 at about 11:00 p.m. Parks was the only victim in this series of disappearances to vanish outside of Washington. Years later, Bundy suggested that he had changed locations to see if he could prevent police from connecting this abduction to those in Washington.

Bundy varied his pattern again when he abducted Brenda Carol Ball on June 1. Ball, who was 22, disappeared after leaving a bar in the Seattle area around 2:00 a.m. Ball was the only woman in the series of disappearances who was not abducted from a college campus. Bundy was again attempting to prevent police from making a connection between the disappearances.

Less than two weeks later, Bundy returned to a college environment. At about 1:00 a.m. on June 11, he abducted Georgann Hawkins. The abduction occurred as Hawkins walked down an alley from a fraternity house near the University of Washington to her sorority house, which was only about 200 yards (180 m) away.

FAMILY EFFORTS

Families of the abducted women took active roles in the search for information. Rancourt's family traveled from their home in Alaska to Central Washington State's campus as police investigated her disappearance. The family stayed in dorm rooms on the campus, and they traveled to other parts of Washington to seek additional help. Parks's family offered a $500 reward, equivalent to about $3,200 in 2024, for information about her disappearance.[2] Sparks's father followed reports of the abductions and saved newspaper articles about them. Even though Sparks was not abducted, her father immediately suspected a connection between her attack and the other women's disappearances.

Connecting the Cases

The six disappearances had taken place in five different towns, which meant several police departments were conducting investigations. There was little evidence from any of the crimes and few leads. Police also had not found any of the women.

After Hawkins's abduction, dozens of officers from several Washington police departments met on the campus of Evergreen State College for a conference to discuss the disappearances. As investigations progressed, similarities in the various disappearances began to emerge. For example, the victims were all close in age and had similar physical appearances. All the missing women were between the ages of 18 and 22. They were all white, described as attractive, and had long blond or brown hair.

Police also observed that most of the disappearances occurred on college campuses. Officers included Parks in this observation even though she went missing from Oregon rather than Washington. The change of location had not confused police as Bundy thought it might. Ball's disappearance was an exception, and police did not connect her case as quickly as they did the others.

When police continued to interview people who had been near the locations of the disappearances, another

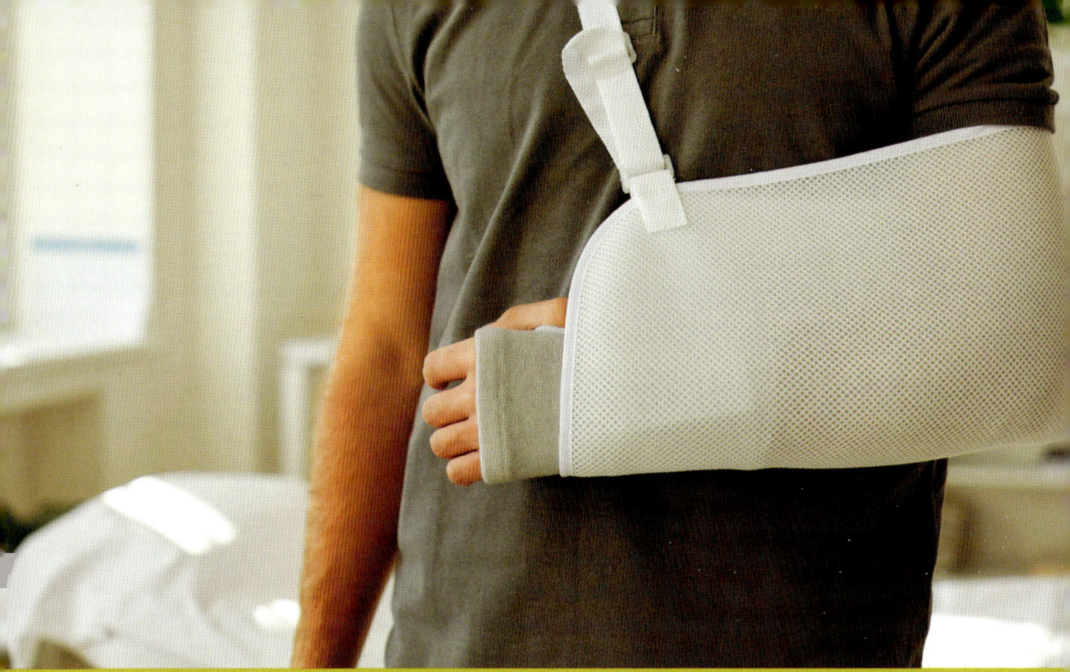

Bundy worked for a medical supply company for some time. He stole items such as casting plaster and crutches, which he later used to fool his victims.

common detail emerged. Several people reported seeing or speaking to a man with his leg in a cast or his arm in a sling. This man would ask for help carrying items such as books to his car, a Volkswagen Beetle. Police believed this man could be their suspect. However, they did not know his identity.

Disappearances in Broad Daylight

On Sunday, July 14, many people were spending the summer day at Lake Sammamish, a state park with hiking trails, beaches, and sports areas. Bundy arrived at the park in his Volkswagen Beetle. He wore one arm in a cast and sling even though his arm was uninjured.

Later, a detective said, "Ted was able to meld into the crowd. He was wearing casual beach-type clothing. He was able to strike up conversations with people."[3]

At about 12:30 p.m., Bundy started chatting with 23-year-old Janice Ann Ott. She had ridden her bike to the lake's beach and was sunbathing. Bundy approached her with a fake story he had devised to lure women to his car. He said he needed help with his sailboat and asked if Ott would go with him to get it. During the conversation, Ott introduced herself as Jan, and Bundy replied, "I'm Ted."[4] Ott left the beach with Bundy, and they headed to the parking lot.

No one saw Ott again after that. However, Bundy returned to the park later in the afternoon and approached another victim. At about 4:30 p.m., Denise Marie Naslund left her boyfriend and the other couple they were with to go to the restroom. She never came back to join her friends.

THE VOLKSWAGEN BEETLE

Bundy bought his first Volkswagen Beetle, a used 1958 model, in his freshman year of college. Bundy purchased the car for $400, which is equivalent to about $4,000 in 2024.[5] Later, he purchased another Beetle, a tan 1968 model. These cars were small and popular in the 1970s, and the Beetle contributed to the wholesome and clean-cut image Bundy presented to several victims.

An Image of the Suspect

In the days and weeks after the Lake Sammamish abductions, police did not find any evidence to suggest who had taken the two women. However, police knew there could be many potential witnesses to the events surrounding their abductions. These were the first of the connected abductions that had occurred at a crowded place during the day.

As police spoke to people who had been at Lake Sammamish on July 14, they learned about a man named Ted who had approached at least five or six other women with the story about needing help with his sailboat.[6] Although police couldn't be sure that Ted was not a fake name, it was one of their only leads. The man did not give a last name to any of these women. Some of them declined to help, but others went with him to his Beetle. When they saw there was no sailboat, the man told them it was at his parents' house nearby. These women declined to get in the car with him.

Witnesses also described the man's appearance and behavior to police. They reported that he was a white man in his twenties with wavy brown hair and a clean-shaven face. He was polite, well-spoken, handsome, and well-dressed.

Bundy's Volkswagen Beetle was once displayed at the Crime Museum in Washington, DC. It was later moved to Alcatraz East Crime Museum in Tennessee.

Tips from the Public

Police released a composite sketch to the public, along with information about the car witnesses had described, and news sources printed it. By this time, there was media coverage and growing public concern about the series of disappearances. Police encouraged people to contact them with any relevant information about the suspect.

On July 22, one of Kendall's coworkers showed her a clipping of the sketch from the *Seattle Times*. Kendall got an uneasy feeling when she noticed similarities between her boyfriend and the drawing. Her suspicion grew when she considered other things she had noticed throughout the year that made her uneasy. For instance, in Bundy's apartment, she had found women's clothing, crutches, and plaster to make casts.

Kendall called the police anonymously, but she did not provide Bundy's last name. Other people acquainted with Bundy also saw the sketch and contacted police. Among these callers were one of Bundy's psychology professors and a previous employer.

These calls were just a few of many reports about potential suspects. At the time, police were receiving hundreds of reports every day. These included reports from other wives and girlfriends who were suspicious of their partners.

There were no more abductions in Seattle after police released the composite sketch. Bundy worked through the summer at the Washington State Department of Emergency Services. There, Bundy began a friendship with Carole Ann Boone. Bundy and Kendall maintained their relationship, although it was often strained. He prepared to move from Washington to Salt Lake City to study at the University of Utah's law school.

"There was incredible pressure on law enforcement to find the person who was responsible for causing these women to go missing."[7]

–Kathleen McChesney, a detective who investigated the disappearances

CHAPTER 4

A KILLING SPREE

In early September 1974, Detective Robert Keppel arrived at a patch of forest in Issaquah, Washington. The site was about one mile (1.6 km) from Lake Sammamish State Park, where Ott and Naslund had disappeared in July.[1] The King County Police Department, where Keppel worked, had been investigating the Washington abductions ever since Healy disappeared in February. Keppel was there to investigate human bones that two hunters found at the site the previous day.

Police had responded quickly and recovered the skull the hunters found. About 30 feet (9 m) away from the skull, a backbone with ribs attached was also found.[2] Police had taken those remains to the medical examiner's office. The examiner used dental records to identify the skull as belonging to Naslund.

Keppel oversaw the continued search for other remains. A team of volunteers from Explorer Search and

The remains found in Issaquah were about 50 feet (15 m) from a dirt road. Bundy did not go far into the forest to deposit the women's bodies.

Rescue (ESAR) conducted the search. More than 50 ESAR volunteers, many of whom were teenagers, worked for seven days from sunrise to sundown. They crawled over the forest floor through thick vegetation to conduct a thorough search of the area. In total, they recovered 400 additional pieces of bone and other human remains.[3]

Experts again used dental records to identify a jawbone found in the area, which they learned belonged to Ott. Searchers also found pieces of spine and leg bones from a third person. However, without a skull or jawbone from that victim, experts could not learn the person's identity.

The search proved at least three of the missing women had been murdered. But it produced no new evidence connecting the crimes to the police's mysterious suspect known to them only as Ted. Keppel later wrote, "In the history of King County homicide investigation, no murder case had a crime scene with so little evidence as this one."[4]

THE ESAR SEARCH

The ESAR volunteers did not have experience with police investigations before working with Keppel. Their organization searched for and rescued people who became lost in the woods while participating in recreation activities such as hiking. The ESAR group approached the police work by dividing the search area into sections, placing string to mark the boundaries of each section. They moved on their hands and knees to examine each section. Keppel praised their commitment and methods. "The ESAR search techniques proved invaluable for us since we had never been faced with processing this type of outdoor crime scene before," he wrote.[5]

Killing in Utah

Police did not know Bundy had already murdered another woman. A few days before the discovery of the bones in Issaquah, Bundy began the drive from Washington to Salt Lake City, Utah, to begin law school. On this drive, he encountered a woman hitchhiking in Idaho. They rode

Bundy had a normal life outside of his attacks, maintaining relationships with friends who knew nothing about his secret criminal activities.

together for a while in Bundy's Beetle before he struck her in the head, raped her, and strangled her. Bundy left her body in the Snake River and destroyed her identification card so that her name would not be known. Her body was never found.

Law classes started at the University of Utah in the fall, but Bundy rarely attended from early October to early November. During that period of time, Bundy began a new series of abduction and murders. He killed at least four teenagers in these attacks.[6]

On October 2, Nancy Wilcox, a 16-year-old high school junior, disappeared from the Salt Lake City suburb

POLICE CHIEF LOUIS SMITH

Police Chief Smith grieved the loss of his daughter. At the same time, other young women in the Salt Lake City area contacted him because they were worried about the series of abductions and murders. Smith told a local newspaper, "They've called us at all times of the day and night, and some of them have asked me personally to their homes, or they've come to my house. They're all frightened, and this community is very concerned."[8]

of Holladay. Friends reported seeing her in a Volkswagen with a man, but they did not have a description of the man. Police never found Wilcox's body.

About two weeks later, Melissa Smith, a 17-year-old high school senior, disappeared at about 10:00 p.m. Melissa's father, Louis Smith, was the police chief in Midvale, a town near Salt Lake City. Melissa had gone to see a friend at a local pizza restaurant before her disappearance.

On October 27, deer hunters in Summit County, which neighbored Midvale, found Melissa's body hidden in brush about a mile (1.6 km) away from the interstate.[7] The hunters called the police. Melissa's body was unclothed, but there was a knee-high sock wrapped around her neck. Injuries to her body showed she had suffered a skull fracture and had been raped. The blow to her head was likely the cause of her death.

A medical examiner determined that Melissa had likely died two or three days before the hunters discovered her body. This information meant she may have lived for about a week after her abduction. There were no binding marks on Melissa's body to indicate she had been tied up, and there were no signs, such as broken fingernails, to show she had fought her attacker. For these reasons, investigators believed she had been unconscious in the days between her abduction and murder.

On October 31, 17-year-old Laura Ann Aime disappeared. She had been hitchhiking after attending a Halloween party in Orem, Utah, approximately 40 miles (64 km) from Salt Lake City. Weeks later, hikers found her body close to a road in American Fork Canyon.

A Victim Escapes

At about 7:00 p.m. on November 8, 18-year-old Carol DaRonch went to Fashion Place Mall in Murray, another Salt Lake City suburb. Bundy approached her. He pretended to be a police officer, although he was not in uniform. Bundy introduced himself as Officer Roseland rather than Ted.

Bundy told DaRonch that someone had tried to break into her car in the mall's parking lot. He said he needed to take her to the police station to report the incident. DaRonch asked Bundy for his credentials, and he showed

Carol DaRonch later spoke in court about her encounter with Bundy.

her a badge. She also saw that he had handcuffs in the breast pocket of his jacket.

Bundy led DaRonch to his Beetle. She noticed unusual things about the car, including rust patches on the hood, a rip in the back seat, and a missing license plate. DaRonch got into the passenger seat, but she felt uneasy.

Bundy drove away from the mall and stopped at a nearby street corner. DaRonch asked why they had stopped, but Bundy did not respond. He retrieved the handcuffs from his jacket pocket and put them around one of DaRonch's wrists.

DaRonch fought him. She used her free hand to open the car door. Bundy grabbed her arm and neck and threatened to shoot her. Still, DaRonch continued to struggle. She escaped from the car, screaming, and Bundy climbed through the passenger side door after her. She scratched him and held back his arm as he tried to strike her head with a metal object that she believed to be a crowbar.

DaRonch was able to exit the vehicle, and she began running down the street. She waved her arms and jumped up and down to attract an approaching car's attention. The car stopped. The older couple inside, Wilbur and Mary Walsh, had been on their way to the grocery store.

"I have never seen a human being that frightened in my life. She was trembling and crying, and almost weak like she was going to faint, and she was just in a terrible state."[9]

—Mary Walsh, who Carol DaRonch flagged down for help

DaRonch leapt into the car and asked them to take her to the police station. Once there, DaRonch reported the attempted abduction, and she described the attacker and his car. DaRonch was the first of Bundy's victims to escape in the middle of an abduction. Therefore, she was also able to provide, for the first time, a firsthand account of the attacker's methods.

A Second Attempt

When DaRonch escaped, Bundy got back into his vehicle and drove away. He traveled 20 miles (32 km) to Viewmont High School in the city of Bountiful to search for another victim.[10] People were at the school that evening to see a play.

It was about 7:30 p.m. when Bundy stopped the drama teacher, 24-year-old Raelynn Shepherd, in the hallway. He asked her to come to the parking lot with him to identify a car. He said he needed to find its owner. Shepherd replied that she was busy. He asked her again a short time later, and again, she refused. Shepherd saw Bundy leave the school building at about 9:15 p.m.

The play ended just after 10:30 p.m., and Shepherd again saw Bundy in the auditorium. He was breathing loudly, and his hair was disheveled. Shepherd didn't know it yet, but in the time between sightings, 17-year-old Debra Jean Kent had gone missing from the school's parking lot. Debra's parents had given her their car keys so she could leave the play to pick up her younger brother from a nearby roller skating rink. Police did not find her body in the weeks or months following her disappearance.

Finding Remains

After Debra's disappearance, Bundy seemed to go quiet for the fall and early winter. However, on January 12, 1975, a 23-year-old nurse named Caryn Campbell disappeared from a ski lodge in Snowmass, Colorado. On February 17, a person passing along Owl Creek Road a few miles from the ski lodge found her unclothed body in the snow. An autopsy found Campbell had suffered blows to her head. She had died within hours of her disappearance.

Two weeks later, on March 1, King County police back in Washington received a phone call about another skull found in a wooded area. Two students from Green River Community College discovered the skull on Taylor

DENTAL RECORDS

Experts called forensic odontologists use dental records to identify crime victims whose bodies cannot be identified through other methods. When a victim is abducted, police may obtain dental records from that person's dentist or family. These records contain X-ray images of the teeth, along with a history of dental work, such as cavity fillings. Forensic odontologists examine the records to determine unique features of the teeth, including their size, shape, and arrangement in the bone. If a skull or jawbone of the victim is available, experts can compare these features to the remains to identify the person.

Snowmass is a popular skiing village less than 10 miles (16 km) from Aspen. Bundy had traveled to the area during his law school's winter break.

Mountain while they were doing classwork for a forestry project. The skull's location was approximately ten miles (16 km) from the Issaquah location where Ott and Naslund's remains had been found the previous year.[11]

Detective Keppel and an ESAR team searched the Taylor Mountain site. They found skull and jaw bones from four additional victims, but they did not find bones from other body parts.[12] Keppel and other officers began to suspect the killer Ted had decapitated these women and left their heads at the Taylor Mountain site away from the rest of their remains. However, they could not yet prove this theory.

Experts determined the skull and jaw bones belonged to Healy, Rancourt, Parks, and Ball. These discoveries, combined with those from the Issaquah site, meant police had identified remains from six of the eight women abducted in Washington. They had not yet identified remains of Hawkins or Manson.

CHAPTER 5

ARRESTED IN UTAH

Discovery and identification of the six women's remains confirmed to Washington police that the cases were related and that one person was responsible for all of them. After the discoveries, Washington police created a Ted Task Force. Keppel, his partner Roger Dunn, and another King County detective named Kathleen McChesney formed the core of this group.

The task force detectives had a list of 3,500 names they had gathered from public tips, as well as large amounts of paperwork and case files to organize.[1] Their goal was to narrow the list to 100 of the most likely suspects. The detectives used a computer program to help them determine who to investigate more thoroughly. The program found names that were repeated most often across lists of potential suspects.

The Ted Task Force also had contact with police from Utah and Colorado who were continuing to investigate

Bundy's case was one of the first that Keppel investigated with the King County Sheriff's Office.

the abductions and murders in their states. Police from the three states did not yet have evidence to prove a connection. However, some of the officers believed there was one, and they kept in contact as the disappearances and murders continued.

Four More Murders

After Campbell's murder in Colorado, Bundy returned to Utah. He took his exams at law school. He also dedicated himself to attending more classes than he had in the fall.

Although people had called the tip line about Bundy before, police initially did not view him as a likely suspect because he was a law student without a criminal record.

Unknown to Bundy, Kendall had called Salt Lake County police and spoken to a detective in January. This was her second report about Bundy. She identified him as a possible suspect in the search for Ted. She had heard about the Utah abductions and murders. Kendall also gave the police her own name, gaining courage since her last anonymous call. Kendall's was not the only call the police had received about Bundy. The task force added his name to their list of the top 100 people to continue investigating.

In early March, Bundy learned the news that police had discovered remains on Taylor Mountain. Then on March 14, he left on another trip to Colorado. In the next four months, he traveled to and from Salt Lake City several times, and at least four more women and girls disappeared.

Julie Cunningham, a 26-year-old ski instructor, vanished from Vail, Colorado, the night of March 15. On April 6, 24-year-old Denise Oliverson disappeared in Grand Junction, Colorado, while bicycling from her home to her parents' home. On May 6, 12-year-old Lynette Dawn Culver vanished after leaving her junior high school in Pocatello, Idaho, at lunchtime. On June 27, 15-year-old Susan Curtis went missing from a youth conference at Brigham Young University in Provo, Utah. Although police investigated, they did not find any of these victims' bodies.

A Traffic Stop

Sergeant Bob Hayward was returning home from his shift between 2:00 and 3:00 a.m. on August 16. Sergeant Hayward was a Utah Highway Patrol Officer.

While Hayward was parked in front of his house, he saw a Volkswagen Beetle slowly drive by. The car's headlights were not turned on.

Ten minutes later, Hayward received a police radio call for backup assistance, and he pulled away from his house to respond. Soon, he caught sight of the Beetle again. It sped away. Sergeant Hayward was suspicious, and he followed the vehicle rather than responding to the earlier radio call. The Beetle's driver ran two stop signs before pulling into a gas station and getting out of the car.

Hayward put out a call for backup assistance and then approached the man and asked for his driver's license. Hayward read the man's name from the license: Theodore Robert Bundy. The license also showed he did not live in Sergeant Hayward's neighborhood. Bundy's address was across town.

Sergeant Hayward found it strange that Bundy had been driving around slowly in the early morning hours in a neighborhood far from his own. In addition, Bundy had committed the traffic violations of driving without headlights and running stop signs. Sergeant Hayward instructed Bundy to stand next to the police car while the officer shone his flashlight into the Beetle. Sergeant Hayward saw the passenger seat lying in the back seat

Hayward had no idea that his routine traffic stop would catch a murderer.

rather than in its proper place. He saw a duffel bag where the passenger seat should have been and a crowbar.

Backup officers, including Detective Daryle Ondrak from the Salt Lake County Sheriff's Office, arrived on the scene and conducted a more thorough search of the car and the duffel bag. The search uncovered handcuffs, an ice pick, rope, strips torn from a sheet, gloves, a ski mask, and a mask made of pantyhose with holes for the eyes and mouth. The collection of items seemed to be burglary tools.

Bundy told police that he was in the neighborhood because he had gotten lost driving home from a movie called *The Towering Inferno*. While still at the scene, police

FORENSIC SPOTLIGHT

Computer-Assisted Suspect Tracking

The Ted Task Force worked with the county's computer experts to create a software application that would help them record, manage, and cross-check suspect information. At the time, police had never before used this type of technology to investigate suspects. People in the department were skeptical about whether it would work.

It took months of work for the Ted Task Force's program to produce a list of suspects, in part because computers in the early to mid-1970s were much slower than they are today.

The task force created lists of people in categories it believed might include the perpetrator, including the 3,500 names gathered from public tips, registered Volkswagen owners, and victims' classmates. The computer program determined which names appeared most frequently across the lists.

Only 25 people appeared on at least four lists of suspects.[2] One of the names was Theodore Bundy. Police were astonished when they learned that a Ted Bundy had been caught in Utah. It seemed the computer program had worked exactly as designed.

Law enforcement agencies continue to use computer programs to determine and track suspects in crimes. Policing practices have evolved to use new technologies, such as artificial intelligence (AI). AI programs use information from the internet to gather data about criminals and crime scene locations. These new technologies are faster and more powerful than early computer-assisted suspect tracking applications.

checked to see if *The Towering Inferno* had shown that night. It had not. Police arrested Bundy on the scene for evading an officer. He was brought to jail, but he soon left on bail.

Building a Case

A few days later, Ondrak brought up Bundy's arrest in a regular weekly meeting for local detectives. He mentioned finding the collection of what seemed to be burglary tools, but he also added, "He's not just your ordinary prowler. Some of the stuff we found in his car is obviously for tying someone up. I don't know. Bundy is the strangest man I've ever met."[3]

Ondrak's statement stood out to Detective Jerry Thompson. Thompson also worked in the Salt Lake County Sheriff's Office. He had been investigating the Utah abductions and murders, including the attempted abduction of DaRonch. Thompson returned to his office to review the information he had about Bundy. Thompson's partner, Detective Ben Forbes, called King County Police. He learned that Bundy was still under investigation on the Ted Task Force's list of 100 suspects.

On August 21, Ondrak arrested Bundy again. Utah police had gotten a warrant to arrest him for possession of burglary tools. Bundy consented to a search of his apartment that same day. In the apartment, Thompson found a brochure with an advertisement for the November 1974 high school play Debra Kent had attended. He found a guide about Colorado ski resorts, including the lodge where Campbell disappeared.

In addition, Thompson found Bundy's gas station credit card bill. Investigators would be able to use the card number from the bill to locate the dates and locations of Bundy's gas purchases. The information could help to establish whether Bundy had been in certain areas when attacks occurred.

Finally, Thompson photographed Bundy's Volkswagen Beetle. Thompson observed the rip in the back seat that DaRonch had described. After the search, police took Bundy back to jail.

MISSING ALIBIS

After receiving the call from Forbes, the Ted Task Force communicated with Kendall. McChesney conducted several interviews with her. Kendall told McChesney about times when Bundy had declined to go out with her or skipped scheduled plans. These instances aligned with dates and times when disappearances had occurred. For example, on June 1, 1974, the day Ball disappeared, Bundy unexpectedly failed to attend the baptism ceremony for Kendall's daughter. Later, Keppel wrote that Bundy could never produce an alibi for the dates and times of victims' disappearances. All other suspects on the task force's list had alibis.

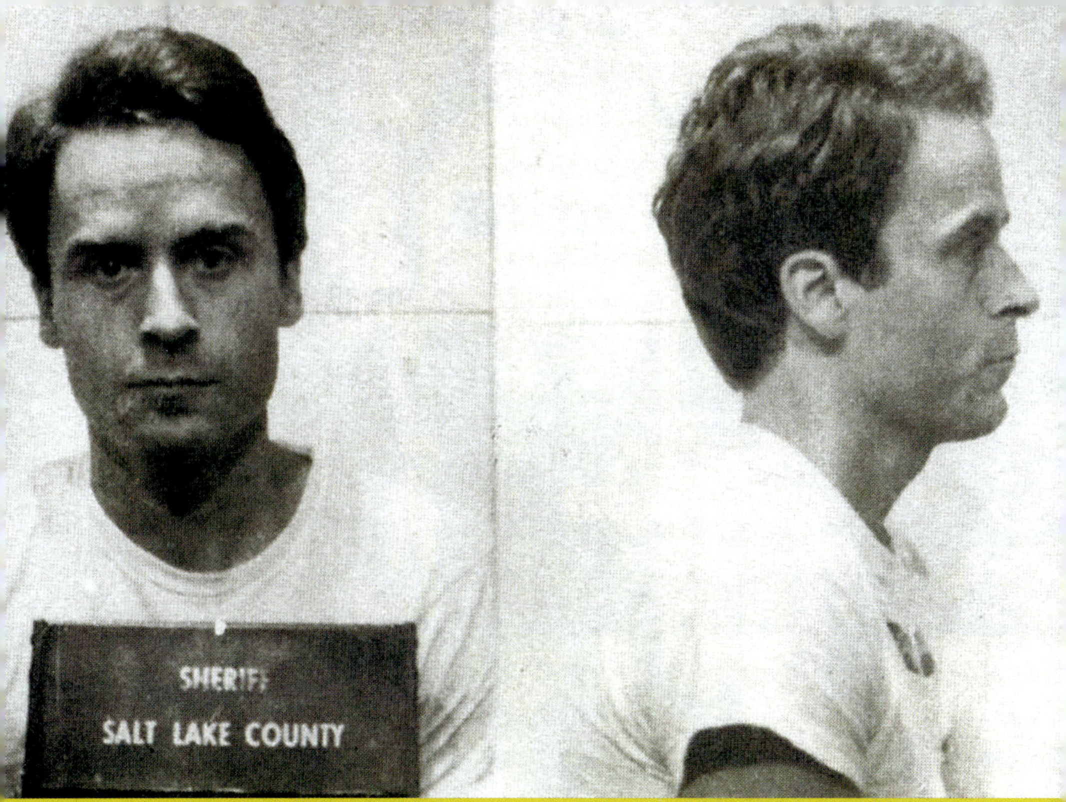

Bundy had a mug shot taken after his October arrest.

He left a few hours later on bail. Police continued to follow Bundy's movements and build their case.

Identified

In early September, Thompson showed DaRonch the photographs he had taken of the Beetle. She said the car resembled the one her attacker drove. Around that same time, Thompson learned Bundy had purchased gas on the same days and in the same areas where Campbell and Cunningham had disappeared.

The Ted Task Force in Washington also referenced Bundy's credit card bills and other financial records.

The group's checks produced evidence that Bundy had traveled from Seattle to the areas where Rancourt and Parks disappeared.

On October 2, by court order, Bundy stood in a lineup with seven other men. DaRonch viewed the lineup and identified Bundy as her attacker. Drama teacher Raelynn Shepherd and one of Debra Kent's classmates also viewed the lineup and identified Bundy as the man they had seen at Viewmont High School the night Debra disappeared.

After the lineup, police arrested Bundy for DaRonch's kidnapping and attempted assault. Eventually he was able to post bail and return home while he awaited trial. Despite charges in DaRonch's case, police did not yet have sufficient evidence to charge Bundy with Debra's disappearance or the abductions and murders of other victims.

"I really couldn't believe it was possible. He was too quiet, too intelligent, too much a nice guy, too much a gentleman to have possibly done anything like that."[4]

—Warren Dodge, a childhood friend of Bundy's, reacting to Bundy's arrest

Thompson, Keppel, and Mike Fisher, an investigator leading the work on Campbell's murder case, met in person with other police and prosecutors to continue comparing their cases. They also discussed new evidence as it emerged. For instance, in a search of Bundy's Beetle after his October arrest, police found hair that matched Campbell's and Smith's.

The DaRonch Trial

Bundy's trial for kidnapping DaRonch began on February 23, 1976, in Salt Lake City. The trial lasted five days. During that time, DaRonch and Bundy both testified.

On March 1, Bundy was found guilty of kidnapping DaRonch. He was sentenced to one to 15 years in prison.[5] It would be up to the parole board to determine how much of that sentence Bundy would serve.

Bundy was held in Utah State Prison. During this time, Bundy maintained contact with his friend from the Department of Emergency Services, Carole Ann Boone. The two exchanged letters and became close.

EXAMINING HAIR

The outside layer of a strand of hair is called the cuticle. The cells that make up the cuticle overlap one another and create patterns that look like scales. Analysts use microscopes to examine these patterns and other details. If a strand's pattern matches that of another sample, the hairs are likely from the same person. Investigators can use microscopic hair analysis to build cases and as evidence in court.

Bundy prepared to serve as his own defense lawyer during his murder trial.

A Murder Charge

In October, Colorado police filed charges against Bundy for the murder of Caryn Campbell. In addition to the gas station credit card records and the hair found in Bundy's car, Fisher had located a new witness who reported seeing Bundy at the ski lodge the night Campbell disappeared. The witness was able to identify Bundy from groups of photos. Colorado Judge George Lohr determined the evidence was sufficient for a murder charge. The charge meant Bundy would be moved to Colorado for his trial.

In response to the murder charge, Bundy said, "I have never killed, never kidnapped, never desired to injure another human being." He added, "I am prepared to use every ounce of my strength to vindicate myself."[6] In late January 1977, Fisher and other officials traveled to Utah to extradite Bundy to Colorado.

IN THE COURTROOM

The media covered Bundy's arrest and legal proceedings closely, and the trial drew many people to the courtroom. Bundy's mother and stepfather attended the proceedings to support him. They trusted his claims that he was innocent. Toward the end of the trial, Kendall, who continued to have a complicated relationship with Bundy, also arrived to support him. Others in attendance supported the prosecution. Among these were Melissa Smith's father and Debra Kent's family, even though this trial did not cover either of their cases.

CHAPTER 6

ON THE RUN

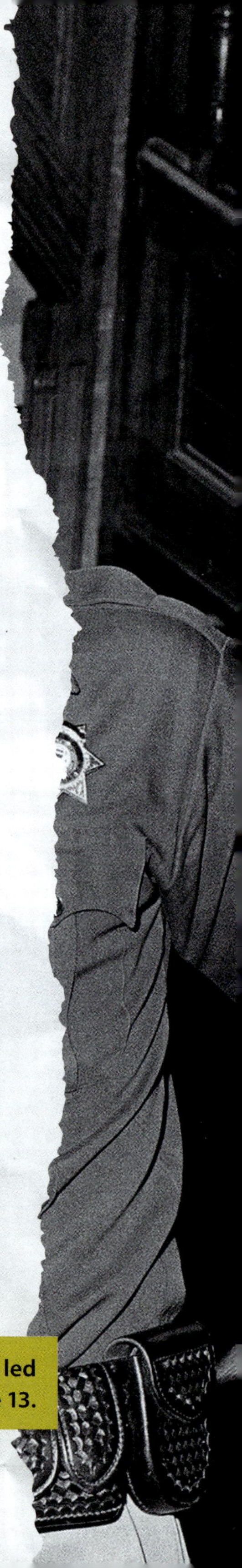

It was after Bundy's extradition to Colorado that he escaped from jail, only to be arrested once again on June 13, 1977. Police took Bundy back to the Garfield County Jail. His trial for Campbell's murder continued to approach.

Before the end of the year, Bundy requested that the court change the location for the trial. Bundy believed he would not have a fair trial in Aspen because his escape had attracted so much attention. Judge Lohr allowed the change and ruled that the trial would take place in Colorado Springs, Colorado. The Colorado Springs prison had

Bundy smiled for a photograph as he was led back to jail following his capture on June 13.

Before his second escape, Bundy piled books on his bed and covered them with a blanket to trick passing prison guards into thinking he was asleep.

tighter security than the Garfield County Jail. Rather than face the transfer to the more secure facility, Bundy decided to try a second escape.

Escaping from Colorado

Bundy's jail cell in Garfield County had a light fixture in the ceiling that needed repair. Without proper welding, the light fixture hung loosely, revealing a hole in the ceiling. Over the next six months, Bundy prepared to use the hole as a path to escape.

With a small saw he had gotten from another prisoner, Bundy cut around the light fixture so that he was able to pull it from the ceiling and access the hole behind it. After losing weight during his first escape, Bundy lost about 30 additional pounds (14 kg) to help him fit through the small opening.[1] He practiced climbing through the hole. He then traveled along the crawl space above the ceiling in search of an exit. He discovered a route to an apartment located inside the prison. The chief jailer lived there. Bundy returned the light fixture back to its proper place after each of his practice runs.

In the night and early morning hours between December 30 and December 31, 1977, Bundy made his escape. He crawled along the path he had chosen. When he arrived at the apartment, Bundy determined the guard and his wife were not there. He broke a hole in the ceiling over the closet, climbed down, and took some of the guard's clothing to change into. After that, he left through the front door of the jail.

WARNINGS FROM OTHER INMATES

Some of the other Garfield County Jail inmates heard noises as Bundy moved through the cramped ceiling spaces above their cells. They reported these noises to jail staff, but staff did not take any additional steps to secure Bundy or his cell. When Mike Fisher, an investigator in the Colorado State Attorney's Office, learned of the reports, he contacted jail staff several times because he believed Bundy would pose a threat to the public if he escaped. Some of the staff were later fired for failing to take action to prevent the escape.

Guards discovered he was missing at about noon on December 31. By that time, Bundy had left the area.

A Cross-Country Fugitive

Outside the prison, Bundy walked in the snow until he located a car he could steal. He drove the stolen car for about 40 miles (64 km) until it broke down.[2] From there, he hitchhiked to Vail, Colorado. In Vail, he took a bus to Denver, Colorado. Bundy flew from Denver to Chicago, Illinois. At that time, passengers did not need to present identification to travel on airplanes. After landing in Chicago, Bundy took a train to Ann Arbor, Michigan.

Bundy spent a few days in Ann Arbor, a college town where he did not attract much attention, even while radio reports covered his escape. Bundy decided not to remain in the area for long. He used the University of Michigan's library to research other college towns where he could go.

HELP FROM A STRANGER

Andy Leyba was driving home from his job as a coal miner early on the morning of December 31, 1977, when a man on the road waved to him for help. It was snowing out, and Leyba observed that the man had no jacket. Leyba said to himself, "If I don't pick this guy up he's going to freeze."[3] As Leyba got close to his destination, he let the man out and gave the man his jacket, which had been a Christmas gift from his wife. Days later, Leyba recognized a picture of Bundy in the news as the man he helped.

Bundy decided on Tallahassee, Florida, where Florida State University was located. He stole a car from an auto shop and drove from Michigan to Atlanta, Georgia. There, he abandoned the stolen car and took a bus to Florida. On January 7, 1978, he arrived in Tallahassee.

Life in Tallahassee

Upon arrival, Bundy rented a room in the Oaks, a boarding house close to Florida State University's campus, using a fake name. For the most part, he was able to go about his activities without attracting attention. Bundy and his crimes were not as well known in other parts of the country as they were in Washington, Utah, and Colorado.

Right away, Bundy returned to some of his old patterns in Tallahassee. Without a job, he relied on his habit of stealing to obtain cash and credit cards to pay for the things he needed. He also stole the keys from a van parked at the university to make a copy of them for later use. He stole another vehicle's license plate. Soon, he returned to murder.

The Chi Omega House Attacks

Nita Neary was a member of the Florida State University chapter of Chi Omega. At 3:00 a.m. on January 15, Neary's boyfriend dropped her off at the sorority house. They had been out on a date.

Neary entered the house through an unlocked sliding glass door. While she was still downstairs, Neary heard a noise that sounded like someone falling, followed by footsteps from someone running in the hallway upstairs. Neary assumed the noises had come from another member of the sorority. However, the person who ran downstairs was a man, not one of Neary's sorority sisters. The man stopped at the front door and ducked down. Neary observed that he was a young, thin, white man carrying a large tree branch.

The man exited the front door. Neary was unsure what had just happened. She went upstairs to wake her roommate, along with the president of the sorority house.

"I think the bite mark, itself, is indicative of the primal rage that Mr. Bundy must've been in at the time that he committed those murders. It was just a total homicidal rage."[4]

—Larry Simpson, a prosecutor in the Chi Omega case

As the women were talking, Karen Chandler stumbled from her room. Blood streamed from wounds on her head. Chandler could hardly speak to ask for help.

The women quickly called the police. While they waited for officers to arrive,

Neary later testified as a witness of the Chi Omega attacks. She identified Bundy as the man she had seen fleeing from the house.

they discovered another victim of the attack. Chandler's roommate, Kathy Kleiner, sat in her bed covered in blood from severe injuries.

The man had also attacked two other women, Margaret Bowman and Lisa Levy, in two separate bedrooms. He struck them with the tree branch, strangled them, and sexually assaulted them. He bit Levy, leaving a mark on her body, which police photographed during their investigation. Levy and Bowman both died from their injuries.

Bowman, *right*, was 21 years old when Bundy killed her. Levy, *left*, was 20.

A Bloody Path

Bundy committed the attacks on all four women in the Chi Omega House within 30 to 45 minutes. But they would not be his last of the evening. He left the Chi Omega house and searched for another victim. At about 4:00 a.m., Bundy entered Cheryl Thomas's bedroom a few blocks away from the Chi Omega house. Thomas was also a student at Florida State University. She was studying dance.

Bundy began to beat Thomas with the branch. Thomas's neighbors heard the blows and tried calling her telephone. When she did not answer, they called the police. Officers found Thomas unconscious in her bedroom, covered in blood, with similar injuries as the women at Chi Omega. Bundy, however, had left the scene. Responders transported Thomas to the hospital, where she spent several days in a coma. She regained consciousness and survived, though she had severe and lasting injuries.

Thomas could not give a description of the person who attacked her because the attack occurred when she was asleep. Neary had seen him, though, and described him for a police sketch. At the scene, police also found a mask that the attacker had made from pantyhose with holes cut out for his eyes. Strands of hair stuck to the mask, which law enforcement could use as evidence to help identify the attacker.

CONVERSATION AT THE OAKS

Bundy returned to the Oaks after escaping from Thomas's room. At about noon, just hours after committing the attacks, Bundy joined a conversation with other residents who had heard about the murders and assaults. One resident said he thought the attacker was someone who was "now probably hiding out real scared." Bundy gave a different opinion. He did not reveal himself as the attacker, but he said the person was an experienced killer who likely had escaped. He said the attacks had a "professional" quality about them.[5]

CHAPTER 7

THE LAST MURDER

Police in Florida were shocked by the scope of the crimes committed on January 15. Ken Katsaris, the sheriff of Leon County, where Tallahassee is located, said, "How could that person go just a few blocks and strike again?"[1] Soon, Katsaris received a phone call from police in Colorado.

Katsaris knew about Bundy's crimes on the other side of the country. However, he did not think the pattern in those crimes resembled the details of the Tallahassee cases. Katsaris wrote down Bundy's name. "But I did not think that the method of operation of *this* case was anything near similar, except for an attack on girls. . . . So I did not take [the connection to Bundy] at that time as serious," Katsaris said.[2]

Colorado police had also been in touch with the Federal Bureau of Investigation (FBI) since Bundy's escape from Garfield County Jail. The FBI had assisted in earlier

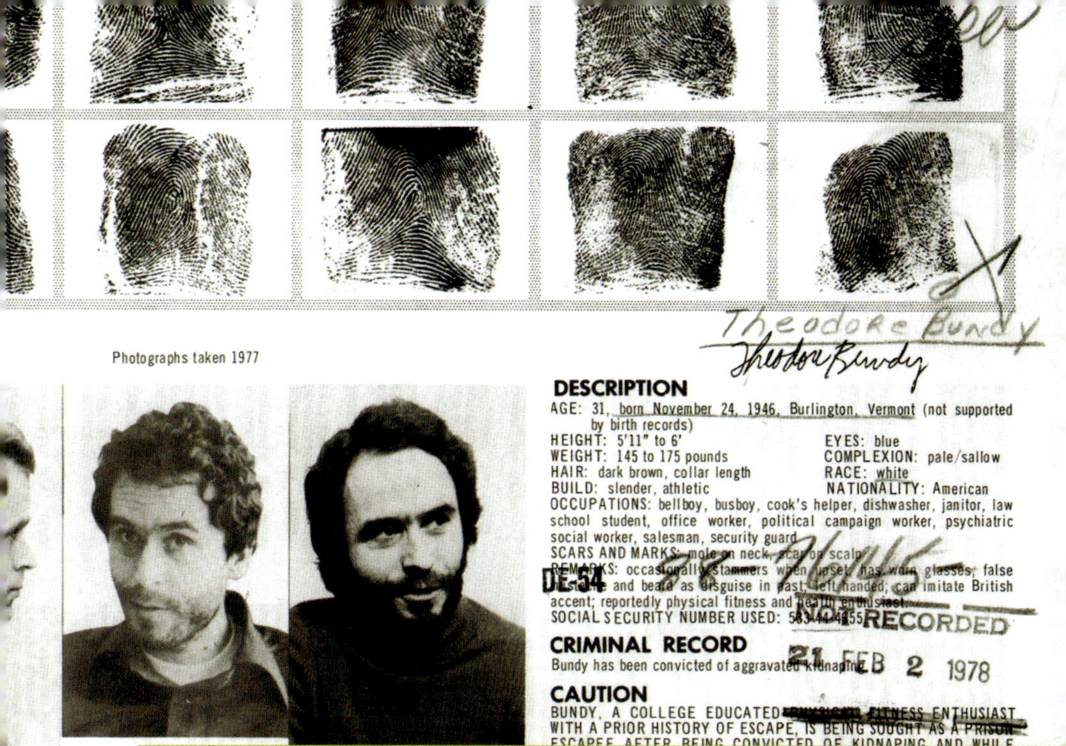

The FBI created a poster with Bundy's photograph, description, and charged crimes.

searches for Bundy. On February 10, 1978, the FBI added Bundy's name to its list of Ten Most Wanted Fugitives.

A Young Victim

At about 8:00 a.m. on Thursday, February 9, Kimberly Leach's mother dropped Kimberly off at school. The girl was a 12-year-old seventh grader at Lake City Junior High School. That Thursday, Kimberly told her physical education teacher she needed to return to homeroom to get her purse, which she had forgotten. Once she retrieved her purse, she began the walk back to class. The walk was not far, only about 250 feet (90 m), but it

Kimberly was a shy student, but she had recently been elected as the runner-up queen for the school's upcoming Valentine's Day dance.

required Kimberly to leave through the back exit of one building and walk outside.[3] There was a street only 15 feet (5 m) from the exit.[4]

As Kimberly made the walk, Bundy approached her and led her to his stolen van. A man passing by saw Bundy holding Kimberly's arm as they walked. The witness thought Bundy was Kimberly's father, who had needed to pick her up early from school.

Once they left school grounds, Bundy beat Kimberly, raped her, and strangled her. He left her unclothed body in an abandoned shed in the woods near Suwannee River State Park, 32 miles (51 km) from Kimberly's school. Bundy returned to Tallahassee by 6:30 p.m. that same day.[5]

A Surprising Capture

Police in the Lake City area assembled a task force of about 100 members and launched an extensive search for Kimberly.[6] Meanwhile, Bundy spent the next few days after Kimberly's murder in Tallahassee. He stole two more cars, one of which was an orange Volkswagen Beetle. On February 12, Bundy drove the orange Beetle from Tallahassee to the western part of Florida.

At about 1:30 a.m. on February 15, Bundy was sitting in the Beetle in a parking lot behind a restaurant in Pensacola, Florida. He had been out searching for his next victim. As Bundy waited in the parking lot, Officer David Lee, who was on the routine midnight policing

FAILED ATTEMPT

Before abducting Kimberly, Bundy tried to abduct another girl, 14-year-old Leslie Parmenter, in Jacksonville. Leslie had finished school for the day and was waiting in a shopping center parking lot for her brother to pick her up. Bundy began talking to her. He had driven to the parking lot in the stolen van and disguised his appearance with glasses and a jacket. He had a badge identifying him as fireman Richard Burton. When Leslie's brother arrived, Bundy left.

A NEAR MISS

On February 11, 1978, Officer George Keith Daws was on duty in Tallahassee near Florida State University's campus. Daws was a deputy with the Leon County Sheriff's Department. At approximately 2:00 a.m., Daws saw Bundy tampering with a Toyota. When Daws approached to ask Bundy what he was doing, Daws spotted another car's license plate inside the vehicle. Daws returned to his police car to run a check on the license plate. Bundy sprinted away from the scene before Daws could identify him.

shift, observed him. Bundy drove out of the parking lot without turning on the Beetle's headlights.

Lee drove behind Bundy's car for a few blocks then switched on the blue lights of his police car. Bundy pulled over, and Lee radioed dispatch to run the Beetle's license plate. This check revealed that the car had been stolen in Tallahassee.

Lee ordered Bundy to get out of the car and lie on the ground with his face down and hands out. Bundy did as instructed and seemed to be cooperative. He asked Lee several times, "Officer, what's wrong?"[7] Lee began to handcuff Bundy, but after he secured the cuffs around one wrist, Bundy grew combative. He kicked Lee's feet out from under him, knocking Lee to the ground. When Bundy began to move toward him, Lee fired a shot, and Bundy fled.

Lee ran after him, ordered him to stop, and fired a second shot. Bundy fell to the ground, and Lee approached him, fearing the shot may have injured or killed Bundy. However, the shot had not struck Bundy. As Lee checked on him, Bundy again kicked him and reached for Lee's gun.

The two continued to struggle until finally Lee managed to handcuff both of Bundy's wrists. Lee led Bundy to the police car and asked for his name. Bundy said he was Kenneth Misner, a 29-year-old graduate student at Florida State University. He produced a driver's license with the same name on it as proof.

A Fake Identity

Lee took Bundy to the Pensacola police station, where police found that he had 21 credit cards with 12 different names on them as well as identification connected to at least three Florida State University students.[8] Bundy continued to insist that he was Kenneth Misner and gave police details about his life. He had a birth certificate with Misner's name and birth date on it. He said he had graduated with his bachelor's degree in 1972 and served in the US Air Force before returning to Florida State University for graduate school.

Later in the day on February 15, reporters began looking into Kenneth Misner's background as they researched the arrest. They found Misner's home address in Tallahassee and went to investigate. At the home, they spoke with a man who also said his name was Kenneth Misner. Misner told reporters that he was a graduate student at Florida State University but he had lost his university ID card several weeks ago. After talking with reporters, Misner contacted police to report his stolen identity.

Police confronted Bundy with the new information. Bundy eventually admitted that his name was not Kenneth Misner, but he would not provide his real name. Newspaper articles on February 16 referred to the arrested man as Mr. X. Finally, police made a deal with Bundy. They would give him time on the telephone in exchange for his name, and Bundy agreed. Later on February 16, he told police his name was Theodore Robert Bundy.

"He was very personable, very charismatic, very unalarming, and see, that's the dangerous thing."[9]

—Norman Chapman, an investigator in Pensacola when Bundy was arrested

A Wanted Killer

After Bundy admitted his identity, Lee located the poster from the FBI. Pensacola police matched the photograph and description on the poster to the man Lee had arrested. On the night of February 16, FBI agents confirmed Bundy's identity. They compared fingerprints taken from Bundy in Pensacola to fingerprints they had on file from Bundy's previous arrests. The fingerprints matched.

Less than two months later, on April 7, police discovered Kimberly's body in a shed near Suwannee River State Park. Prosecutors charged Bundy with her murder on July 21, 1978. Kimberly's death was the last of Bundy's murders. Days later, prosecutors charged Bundy with the murders of Bowman and Levy and the attacks on Kleiner, Thomas, and Chandler.

THE REAL KENNETH MISNER

As a college student at Florida State University, Misner ran track and held university records for two- and six-mile distances. Misner served in the US Air Force for four years. He then worked for the Tallahassee recreation department. Misner returned to Florida State University for a graduate degree in the education department. Similar to Bundy, Misner had brown hair, blue eyes, and an athletic build. Misner was alarmed at how much Bundy knew about his life. He worried that reports of his name on the news and in papers would ruin his reputation.

CHAPTER 8

THE KILLER ON TRIAL

Prosecutors in Florida offered Bundy a plea agreement. They would remove the death penalty as a sentencing option if Bundy pleaded guilty and provided a full confession of the murders he committed in Florida. Bundy would spend the rest of his life in prison, but he would not be executed. A defense attorney advised Bundy to accept the deal, but he rejected it in May 1979. The first of Bundy's two murder trials soon began.

An Unusual Trial

Bundy was tried first for the Chi Omega house murders and the attempted murder of Cheryl Thomas. Initially, the trial was set to take place in Tallahassee, where the attacks happened. However, the trial moved to Miami because it was not possible to find an impartial jury in Tallahassee. Jury selection in Miami was finalized on June 30, 1979. Judge Edward Cowart presided over the proceedings.

Bundy was tried separately for the murder of Kimberly Leach and for the Chi Omega attacks.

News media broadcast the pretrial hearings and the trial itself. This live broadcasting was one factor that made the trial unusual. It had only recently become legal to allow television cameras in Florida courtrooms. Bundy's trial was one of the first in United States history to be broadcast across the nation while it happened.

Before the trial, Bundy asked the judge to limit the presence of television cameras during proceedings. The judge denied the request, but Bundy adapted to being on camera. One of his defense attorneys said, "He was very conscious of the camera."[1]

The issue of defense attorneys was another unusual factor in the trial. Bundy wanted to represent himself, which he had planned to do in Colorado. Self-representation is a legal right in the United States, but it is not common in serious felony cases. As the trial grew closer, Bundy agreed to have public defenders help him. A lawyer from a private firm also offered assistance. Even with this aid, Bundy took an active part in court proceedings.

LIFE AFTER ASSAULT

Thomas and Kleiner survived Bundy's attacks, but their lives were changed. Thomas's physical injuries ended her hopes of becoming a professional dancer. However, she eventually taught ballet classes and worked with deaf people. Thomas's own hearing had been impaired by Bundy's blow to her ear.

Kleiner noticed she was afraid of unknown men after the attack. She took a job as a cashier in a lumberyard, where she would see many men, to train herself out of the fear. She said this tactic proved successful. Kleiner went on to have a fulfilling life too.

Evidence and Witness Testimony

Pretrial proceedings began in early July. These hearings did not take place in front of the jury. Their purpose was to determine which pieces of evidence and testimony would be allowed during the trial. During these proceedings, Bundy questioned police involved in his Utah arrests, including Sergeant Hayward. Judge Cowart ruled that evidence from those arrests was outside the scope of the Chi Omega house trial. This meant Bundy's current trial would focus only on the attacks in Tallahassee.

Margaret Good, *left*, was one of Bundy's defense lawyers

The trial began on July 7 in front of a 12-person jury. Prosecutors called Neary as a witness to identify Bundy as the man she saw in the Chi Omega house the night of the attacks. They also called an expert witness, Patricia Lasko, to the stand to testify about the hairs found in the pantyhose mask left in Thomas's bedroom. Lasko testified that the hairs were "exactly like" Bundy's.[2]

Richard Souviron gave evidence about the bite marks on Levy's body. Souviron showed the court a picture of the bite marks. Next, he showed them a picture of Bundy's teeth printed on a clear sheet. Souviron demonstrated that Bundy's teeth aligned with the bite marks by placing the clear sheet over the picture of the bite marks.

Patricia Lasko explained the science of hair identification to the court during Bundy's trial.

Survivors from the attacks also testified as witnesses. They described being attacked in their bedrooms and the injuries they suffered. Lawyers asked each woman if she could identify the attacker, but none could. Neary, however, did identify Bundy.

A Conviction

After the jurors heard the evidence and testimony, they deliberated on the case. In less than seven hours, they found Bundy guilty in the murders of Levy and Bowman as well as the attempted murders of Kleiner, Chandler, and Thomas. The trial then moved to the sentencing phase, when the same jurors would decide whether to recommend the death penalty as Bundy's sentence.

FORENSIC SPOTLIGHT

Bite Mark Analysis

Bite mark analysis is a forensic technique that compares a bite mark on a victim with an impression or photograph of a suspect's teeth. Some experts, such as Richard Souviron at Bundy's trial, say each person's teeth are unique in their shape, placement in the mouth, and other characteristics. These characteristics can be used to match a suspect's teeth with the bite mark on a victim.

However, some experts don't believe this method is valid. One role of the National Institute of Standards and Technology (NIST) is to use research to guide law enforcement practices and policies. A NIST study researched bite mark analyses and concluded that the patterns of human teeth are not unique in every individual, and these patterns do not always show up consistently in bite marks.

The American Board of Forensic Odontology (ABFO) provides guidelines for how bite mark analysis can be effectively and legally used in trial. The ABFO does allow experts to use bite mark analysis as evidence in court. However, experts may only rule that a suspect could have made a bite mark. Experts cannot declare a perfect match or say with certainty that a specific individual was responsible for a mark.

Richard Souviron created a model of Bundy's teeth to use as evidence during the trial.

Jurors heard additional testimony during this phase. Chandler believed the murders of Levy and Bowman warranted a death penalty. During the trial, she said, "Two people dear to me are dead because of him, and I really think he should be too."[3] Bundy's mother was one of the witnesses to testify against the death penalty. She also spoke about Bundy's innocence outside of court, saying, "We know he's not guilty and so do all his friends."[4]

> **"He's remembered as handsome, but he was just an average person—you'd pass him by. He was sitting there, impatient, arrogant, like a bored middle manager, like we were wasting his time."[6]**
>
> *—Kathy Kleiner, a survivor of the Chi Omega attacks, on Bundy's appearance during trial*

The jury decided to recommend the death penalty and gave their decision to Judge Cowart. It would be up to the judge to issue the final sentence. Judge Cowart took the jury's recommendation. On July 31, 1979, Judge Cowart delivered a death penalty sentence. Bundy's response seemed to show his familiar mask of composure. "See you next trial," he said.[5]

The Second Murder Trial

After Bundy's convictions and death sentence in July 1979, he faced another trial for the abduction and murder of

Kimberly Leach. This trial began in January 1980. Similar to the first trial, the second trial was moved from the city of the attack because it would be difficult to find an impartial jury. Instead, the trial took place in Orlando, Florida. Judge Wallace Jopling presided over this trial.

This trial was also televised, but Bundy took a less active role in his defense. Prosecutors called witnesses who had seen the stolen van in areas near Kimberly's school and near where her body was found. The witness who had seen a man leading Kimberly away from her school also testified. He said the man he had seen looked a lot like Bundy.

Evidence for the prosecution also came from Richard Stephens, a serologist from the Florida Department of Law Enforcement. Stephens testified that body fluids found in the van matched Kimberly's blood type and other characteristics of her blood.

BUNDY'S COURTROOM DEMEANOR

During his second trial, Bundy began to lose the cool composure he had kept up throughout the Chi Omega trial. His mask first slipped when a witness picked Bundy out of a lineup. Bundy shouted that the man had lied. When speaking to a friend, Bundy said, "I just can't keep it together anymore. I'm sorry. I'm just starting to lose it. . . . I need some . . . special attention! I demand it!"[7] Bundy barely held himself together for the remainder of the trial.

Body fluids found on Kimberly's clothing matched Bundy's blood type.

Some of the prosecution's strongest evidence came from Mary Lynn Hinson, who worked as a microanalyst in the Florida Department of Law Enforcement. Hinson analyzed clothing fibers. She found fibers matching Kimberly's clothing and purse inside the van Bundy had stolen. Fibers found in Kimberly's socks and jeans also matched Bundy's clothes, which had been found in the stolen van.

After hearing all the evidence, jurors deliberated for seven and a half hours. They returned a guilty verdict on February 7. The trial for Kimberly's murder then moved to the penalty phase.

AN INSANITY DEFENSE

Vic Africano served as Bundy's attorney for his second trial. Africano said he considered whether Bundy might plead not guilty by reason of insanity for the murder of Kimberly Leach and the Chi Omega murders. This legal defense would claim that Bundy had been incapable of knowing his actions were wrong due to severe mental illness. Africano abandoned the idea after consulting a doctor, who was confident that Bundy was mentally ill but did not believe an insanity defense would be successful in court.

A Marriage and Another Death Sentence

Bundy's friend Carole Ann Boone maintained her support

for Bundy over the years, and their friendship had turned into a romantic relationship. Boone appeared as a witness during the penalty phase of the second trial. Bundy took an active role in this part of the trial and questioned Boone himself on February 9.

The two had developed a plan to marry each other in the courtroom. Boone had obtained a marriage license during the first phase of the trial. Under Florida law, if a couple with a marriage license exchanged vows in front of a judge, the marriage became legal.

On the stand, Boone spoke of her feelings for Bundy. He asked, "Do you want to marry me?" Boone replied, "Yes." Bundy then said, "I do hereby marry you."[8] This exchange met Florida's legal requirements for a marriage. The exchange took place in front of the jury. Prosecutors criticized Bundy for using serious court proceedings in this way.

In addition to witnessing the marriage, jurors also heard a statement from Bundy about why he should not not be executed. Jurors deliberated for less than an hour before recommending a death sentence. Again, the final sentencing rested with the judge. Judge Joplin accepted the jury's recommendation, and on February 12, he gave Bundy a death sentence for Kimberly's murder.

CHAPTER 9

CONFESSIONS AND EXECUTION

Bundy's execution was scheduled for March 4, 1986. However, he and his lawyers quickly began to appeal the sentences. Appeals are common in death penalty cases, and they often take years to resolve. A court may overturn the death sentence or the conviction entirely if an appeal is successful.

Bundy's legal team appealed the outcomes of both the Chi Omega trial and the Kimberly Leach trial several times. Bundy claimed that he had not received a fair trial for a variety of reasons, including that grand jury selection was unfair, the trial's change

Some of Bundy's appeals contested the presence of media in the courtroom.

Jurors in Bundy's Chi Omega trial left the courtroom after his sentencing. Many of Bundy's appeals claimed the jurors in his trials had become biased or corrupted.

of venue violated his rights, and he was mentally unfit to stand trial.

In a 1985 appeal, Bundy and his lawyers claimed the judge in the Kimberly Leach trial unfairly allowed testimony from a witness who had undergone hypnosis. Hypnosis was used to help witnesses remember details about their experiences that they may have forgotten or struggled to access. The man who had seen Bundy holding Kimberly's arm outside the girl's school had undergone hypnosis to remember details about the scene.

Although the practice was fairly common at the time, it was also questioned by legal and psychological experts.

In Bundy's case, the witness had undergone hypnosis months after he had seen the incident. Bundy argued that between the incident and the witness's testimony, the media had suggested details he claimed to remember that linked Bundy to Kimberly's disappearance.

The court recognized that hypnosis was a questionable practice. However, the court said "that sufficient evidence does exist, absent the tainted testimony, upon which the jury could have based its conviction of Bundy."[1] Bundy's appeal was once again denied.

Stay of Execution

Desperate to delay his death, Bundy continued trying to overturn his sentence. Polly Nelson, Bundy's new lawyer, helped stay Bundy's execution. During this time, Bundy's appeals went all the way to the US Supreme Court, which heard Bundy's case in 1986.

Bundy's appeal to the US Supreme Court repeated several points that served as the basis for his earlier attempts. The Supreme Court agreed with the lower courts' rulings. In a 2–7 vote, Bundy's appeal was denied.

Although his legal team continued to bring cases to court, Bundy could not escape his sentence. His last stay of execution was denied on January 17, 1989. Bundy's execution was scheduled for January 24.

Confessing until Death

While Bundy was in prison, he gave interviews to several members of the press and law enforcement, totaling more than 150 hours.[2] Two journalists, Stephen Michaud and Hugh Aynesworth, used this material to write two books, *Conversations with a Killer* and *The Only Living Witness*, which report details from Bundy's crimes, arrests, escapes, and imprisonment.

William Hagmaier, a special agent with the FBI's Behavioral Analysis Unit, also conducted interviews with Bundy. He revealed previously unknown details of his crimes to Hagmaier. From these interviews, Hagmaier learned Bundy performed sexual acts with the bodies of his victims. Bundy also spoke about the ownership he felt over women after murdering them. Once he killed someone, Bundy said he felt as though he possessed her and she was a part of him forever.

"I feel Mr. Bundy has not allowed me to get to know him, and I believe there are many significant things about him that remain hidden."[3]

—Dr. Al Carlisle, a psychologist who worked with Bundy in prison

Seattle detective Robert Keppel met with Bundy many times, including for an interview days before Bundy's execution. On January 20, Bundy confessed the location of Georgann Hawkins' remains: the forest in Issaquah. Bundy's confession confirmed that Hawkins was the third, previously unidentified, victim whose remains searchers had found there in 1974.

Bundy continued to confess new details about his crimes, hoping the information would force officials to further delay his execution so more victims could be laid to rest. A few days before his death, Bundy told Keppel, "We need a period of time, 60, 90 days, a few months, systematically going over with everybody, bottom to top, everything I can think of. Get it all down."[4] Bundy was desperate.

BUNDY AND HAGMAIER

Hagmaier interviewed Bundy many times over the course of four years. Hagmaier believed Bundy preferred to speak to him, rather than other FBI agents, because the men were close in age and both married. Bundy felt close to Hagmaier. Hagmaier said Bundy "probably knew more about law enforcement than I did at that point," and the agent wanted to learn from the serial killer.[5] In addition to information about Bundy's crimes and victims, Hagmaier's interviews provided the FBI with insight into the inner workings of serial criminals.

Victims criticized Bundy's confessions. "It was an obvious attempt to save his neck," Janice Ann Ott's father said. "He had plenty of time before this to cleanse his soul."[6]

Ultimately Bundy's final confessions did nothing to prolong his life. Bundy's death sentence was carried out just after 7:00 a.m. on January 24, 1989, in the electric chair at Florida State Prison. Hundreds of people gathered outside to celebrate. When a spokesperson announced that the execution was complete, the crowd cheered. One person lit fireworks.

POSSIBLE CONNECTIONS

Law enforcement and the public have long speculated about Bundy's unidentified victims. One missing person case has sparked debate: that of Ann Marie Burr, an eight-year-old girl who went missing two miles (3.2 km) from Bundy's childhood home in 1961. In an interview with Keppel, Bundy suggested his killings may have begun before the death of Healy, his first confirmed victim, in 1974. True crime fans connect certain cryptic hints in Bundy's confessions with the young girl. However, Bundy maintained his innocence in Ann Marie's case. When Keppel asked about the girl, Bundy said, "No. Absolutely not."[8] Ann Marie's case remains unsolved.

Counting Victims

By the time of his death, Bundy had confessed to at least 28 specific murders.[7] He spoke about victims in Washington, Utah, Colorado, Florida, Oregon, Idaho, and California. Many of these murders had not been previously connected to Bundy. In 2024, some of Bundy's victims remained unidentified.

Criminologists believe that, based on the extent of Bundy's confessions immediately before his execution, the total count of his victims may be much higher. One investigator recalled Bundy saying, "When you find the person that committed these crimes that you think I committed, that person is going to be wanted for murders of women in the three digits in six states."[9] Although the official count remains 28, some experts believe Bundy may have killed more than 100 people.[10]

Bundy's Legacy

Bundy was one of many serial killers who influenced law enforcement practices and criminal tracking systems. While Bundy was alive, Hagmaier met with FBI agent Pierce Brooks, who was working to start the Violent Criminal Apprehension Program (ViCAP) within the FBI's Behavioral Analysis Unit. ViCAP would be a database that helped authorities notice patterns between crimes perpetrated across the country and more quickly identify serial criminals whose crimes were committed in multiple states.

"I deserve certainly the most extreme punishment society has. . . . Society deserves to be protected from me."[11]

–Ted Bundy, shortly before his execution

Zac Efron starred as Bundy in one film adaptation of the serial killer's life and crimes.

Bundy was an example of a killer who might have been caught earlier with the aid of such a database. Hagmaier helped Brooks garner the necessary support for the program, which began in 1985. The database is still used by law enforcement officers today.

Public interest in Bundy's case has persevered long after his execution. The killer's life and crimes have been the subject of at least a dozen true crime TV shows and documentaries, along with countless books and other media. In the media, Bundy is sometimes referred to as the Campus Killer, reflecting the fact that many of his victims were college students he abducted from campuses across the country.

On the thirtieth anniversary of Bundy's execution, Netflix released the docuseries *Conversations with a Killer: The Ted Bundy Tapes*. The show includes interviews with surviving victims and law enforcement involved in the case, along with tapes from Bundy's own confessions. At the same time, the streaming platform released *Extremely Wicked, Shockingly Evil and Vile*. This dramatic film covers Bundy's life from the perspective of Elizabeth Kendall. The movie is based on Kendall's memoir about her life with Bundy, *The Phantom Prince*, which details Kendall's experience falling in love with a charming man who turned out to be a killer.

Bundy's most enduring legacy lives on in his victims and their loved ones. Bundy ended the lives of at least 28 people. He drastically altered the lives of countless others who survived his attacks or were otherwise touched by his crimes.

TRUE CRIME CONTROVERSY

Zac Efron played Bundy in *Extremely Wicked, Shockingly Evil and Vile*. Critics say the film puts too much weight on Bundy's attractiveness and charm, possibly because of its heartthrob lead actor. Surviving victim Kleiner supported the film, saying, "When they do say positive and wonderful things about him . . . that's what [victims] saw, that's what Bundy wanted you to see."[12] Relatives of other victims felt the film kept Bundy's crimes alive in an unnecessary and traumatizing way.

ESSENTIAL FACTS

TIMELINE

- **Nov. 24, 1946:** Theodore Robert Cowell is born in Burlington, Vermont. He later takes the last name Bundy.
- **Jan. 4, 1974:** Bundy attacks Karen Sparks in her bedroom, leaving her gravely injured but alive.
- **Feb. 1, 1974:** Bundy abducts Lynda Ann Healy from her bedroom and murders her.
- **July 14, 1974:** Bundy abducts two women at Lake Sammamish. Police release a composite sketch.
- **Oct. 2, 1974:** Bundy abducts Nancy Wilcox from Holladay, Utah.
- **Nov. 8, 1974:** Bundy attempts to abduct Carol DaRonch, but she escapes and reports the assault to the police.
- **Feb. 23, 1976:** Bundy's trial begins for the kidnapping of Carol DaRonch. On March 1, he is found guilty.
- **Oct. 21, 1976:** Bundy is charged with the murder of Caryn Campbell.
- **June 7, 1977:** Bundy escapes from jail. He stays on the run until June 13, when he is arrested and returned to custody.
- **Dec. 30, 1977:** Bundy escapes a second time. In the following six weeks, he murders three victims.
- **July 31, 1979:** Bundy is sentenced to death. He later receives a second death sentence.
- **Jan. 24, 1989:** Bundy is executed at Florida State Prison.

IMPACT ON SOCIETY

Ted Bundy committed at least 28 confirmed murders and attacked many additional women and girls across seven states throughout the 1970s. He abducted many of his victims at night, often kidnapping women from college campuses then sexually assaulting and murdering them. For other crimes, Bundy created stories to lure women away from safety before attacking them. Bundy was known to be attractive and charming, and these attributes may have helped him perpetrate his crimes.

Bundy was arrested several times and escaped jail twice. During his second escape, Bundy murdered two women and one young girl. After his final capture, Bundy was sentenced to death and executed. During Bundy's imprisonment, the FBI started the Violent Criminal Apprehension Program (ViCAP), which assists law enforcement in connecting cases that occur across state borders. ViCAP aims to help police catch serial criminals such as Bundy. Since his death, the story of Bundy's life and crimes has remained a popular subject for true crime media.

QUOTE

"He was very personable, very charismatic, very unalarming, and see, that's the dangerous thing."

—Norman Chapman, the police chief in Pensacola when Bundy was arrested

GLOSSARY

abduction

The act of taking someone without their consent.

alibi

A defense that an accused person was with another person or people in a different area at the time of a crime.

appeal

A legal proceeding submitted to ask a higher court to review the decision of a lower court.

autopsy

An examination of a dead body to determine the cause of death.

bail

A fee required to temporarily release an accused person from jail until their next court appearance.

compartmentalize

To separate into different categories.

composite sketch

A drawing of a suspect created by an artist using witness descriptions.

deliberate

To carefully consider a decision.

dismember

To cut a body into separate pieces.

extradite

To move a criminal from one state or county to another for trial.

facade

A fake appearance or front.

lineup

A line of people arranged for police or victims to identify a suspect.

microanalyst

A scientist who analyzes the smallest-scale components of compounds.

parole

The supervised release of a prisoner before the full completion of their sentence, after which the person has to maintain good behavior for a certain period of time.

prosecutor

A lawyer who leads the case against a defendant in court.

serologist

A scientist who studies blood or other body fluids.

ADDITIONAL RESOURCES

SELECTED BIBLIOGRAPHY

Michaud, Stephen G., and Hugh Aynesworth. *The Only Living Witness*. New American Library, 1989.

Ramsland, Katherine. *How to Catch a Killer: Hunting and Capturing the World's Most Notorious Serial Killers.* Sterling, 2020.

Sullivan, Kevin M. *The Bundy Murders: A Comprehensive History*. McFarland, 2020.

FURTHER READINGS

Burling, Alexis. *The Son of Sam Killings*. Abdo, 2020.

Mooney, Carla. *Richard Ramirez: The Night Stalker.* Abdo, 2025.

Rosewood, Jack. *The Ultimate Serial Killer Trivia Book: A Collection of Fascinating Facts and Disturbing Details about Infamous Serial Killers and Their Horrific Crimes.* LAK, 2022.

ONLINE RESOURCES

Booklinks
NONFICTION NETWORK
FREE! ONLINE NONFICTION RESOURCES

To learn more about serial killers, please visit **abdobooklinks.com** or scan this QR code. These links are routinely monitored and updated to provide the most current information available.

MORE INFORMATION

For more information on this subject, contact or visit the following organizations:

ALCATRAZ EAST CRIME MUSEUM

2757 Pkwy.
Pigeon Forge, TN 37863
alcatrazeast.com

The Alcatraz East Crime Museum offers exhibits related to famous crimes and criminals, including Ted Bundy. Bundy's Volkswagen Beetle is on display at the museum. This was the vehicle Bundy drove when police arrested him in August 1975.

AMERICAN BOARD OF FORENSIC ODONTOLOGY (ABFO)

410 N. 21st St.
Colorado Springs, CO 80904
abfo.org

The ABFO is a professional organization that oversees the practice of forensic odontology. The group provides guidelines and information about bite mark analysis and dental identification of remains.

THE FBI EXPERIENCE

935 Pennsylvania Ave. NW
Washington, DC 20535
fbi.gov/contact-us/fbi-headquarters/the-fbi-experience

The FBI Experience is located at FBI headquarters in Washington, DC. There, visitors can explore multimedia exhibits and artifacts that showcase the importance of the FBI's work and history.

SOURCE NOTES

CHAPTER 1. JAILBREAK IN COLORADO

1. Stephen G. Michaud and Hugh Aynesworth. *The Only Living Witness*. New American Library, 1989. 182.
2. Michaud and Aynesworth, *The Only Living Witness*, 186.
3. Michaud and Aynesworth, *The Only Living Witness*, 183.
4. "The First Escape, 1977." *Killer in the Archives*, 26 June 2021, killerinthearchives.blog. Accessed 15 May 2024.
5. Michaud and Aynesworth, *The Only Living Witness*, 196.
6. Michaud and Aynesworth, *The Only Living Witness*, 189.
7. Michaud and Aynesworth, *The Only Living Witness*, 190–191.
8. Michaud and Aynesworth, *The Only Living Witness*, 174.
9. Michaud and Aynesworth, *The Only Living Witness*, 195.

CHAPTER 2. BUILDING A FACADE

1. Stephen G. Michaud and Hugh Aynesworth. *The Only Living Witness*. New American Library, 1989. 65.
2. Michaud and Aynesworth, *The Only Living Witness*, 68.
3. Gina Tron. "Who Was Diane Edwards, Ted Bundy's First Girlfriend, and How Did Their Breakup Impact Him?" *Oxygen True Crime*, 24 Jan. 2019, oxygen.com. Accessed 3 July 2024.
4. Michaud and Aynesworth, *The Only Living Witness*, 66.
5. Michaud and Aynesworth, *The Only Living Witness*, 70.
6. Tron, "Who Was Diane Edwards?"
7. Michaud and Aynesworth, *The Only Living Witness*, 71–72.
8. Kevin M. Sullivan. *The Bundy Murders: A Comprehensive History*. McFarland, 2020. 71.

CHAPTER 3. DISAPPEARANCES IN THE NORTHWEST

1. Jill Sederstrom. "Who Was Lynda Ann Healy, Ted Bundy's First Known Victim, and Why Was the Crime Scene 'Unique?'" *Oxygen True Crime*, 31 Jan. 2019, oxygen.com. Accessed 3 July 2024.
2. "Reward Offered for OSU Coed." *Oregon Statesman*, 14 May 1974, newspapers.com. Accessed 3 July 2024.
3. "Witnesses Recall a Man Named 'Ted' at Lake Where Women Were Abducted by Bundy: Part 3" *ABC News*, 16 Feb. 2019, abcnews.go.com. Accessed 3 July 2024.
4. "Witnesses Recall a Man Named 'Ted.'"
5. Stephen G. Michaud and Hugh Aynesworth. *The Only Living Witness*. New American Library, 1989. 68.

6. "Witnesses Recall a Man Named 'Ted.'"
7. "Witnesses Recall a Man Named 'Ted.'"

CHAPTER 4. A KILLING SPREE

1. Robert D. Keppel. *The Riverman*. Pocket, 1995. 9.
2. Keppel, *The Riverman*, 12.
3. Arthur Santana. "Profiler Mined Minds for Clues." *Seattle Times*, 27 June 1999, archive.seattletimes.com. Accessed 3 July 2024.
4. Keppel, *The Riverman*, 18.
5. Keppel, *The Riverman*, 17.
6. Kevin M. Sullivan. *The Bundy Murders: A Comprehensive History*. McFarland, 2020. 96.
7. "Melissa Smith's Body Found; Funeral Held Wednesday." *Jordan Valley Sentinel*, 31 Oct. 1974, newspapers.com. Accessed 29 July 2024.
8. Bill Beecham. "Fear Grips Young Women after N. Utah Killings." *Ogden Standard-Examiner*, 3 Dec. 1974, newspapers.com. Accessed 3 July 2024.
9. "Trial Transcript: Mary and Wilbur Walch, 1976." *Killer in the Archives*, 8 Dec. 2019, killerinthearchives.blog. Accessed 3 July 2024.
10. Sullivan, *The Bundy Murders*, 109.
11. Ann Rule. "High Promises, Some Mixed Reviews." *Miami News*, 23 Oct. 1980, newspapers.com. Accessed 29 July 2024.
12. Keppel, *The Riverman*, 33–36.

CHAPTER 5. ARRESTED IN UTAH

1. Robert D. Keppel. *The Riverman*. Pocket, 1995. 67.
2. Keppel, *The Riverman*, 72.
3. Steven Winn and David Merrill. "Bundy Escapes: 'The Oldest Trick . . .'" *Morning News* [Wilmington, DE], 8 Jan. 1980, newspapers.com. Accessed 3 July 2024.
4. Stephen G. Michaud and Hugh Aynesworth. *The Only Living Witness*. New American Library, 1989. 161.
5. Kevin M. Sullivan. *The Bundy Murders: A Comprehensive History*. McFarland, 2020. 189.
6. "Guilty as Charged." *Orlando Sentinel*, 24 Dec. 1978, newspapers.com. Accessed 3 July 2019.

CHAPTER 6. ON THE RUN

1. "Photos: The Things He Left Behind, 1977." *Killer in the Archives*, 12 Nov. 2019, killerinthearchives.blog. Accessed 3 July 2024.

SOURCE NOTES CONTINUED

2. Erin Odell. "Ted Bundy: Could His Killing Spree Have Been Stopped Cold in Colorado?" *Coloradoan*, 7 Feb. 2019, coloradoan.com. Accessed 29 July 2024.

3. Alex Zorn. "Bundy's Escape Forever a Part of Garfield County History." *Aspen Times*, 16 Feb. 2019, aspentimes.com. Accessed 3 July 2024.

4. Jeca Taudte, Gwen Gowen, and Enjoli Francis. "Chi Omega Survivor of Ted Bundy Murders: 'I Was Asleep' When Evil Opened Door 'And Attacked Me.'" *ABC News*, 13 Feb. 2019, abcnews.go.com. Accessed 3 July 2024.

5. US Department of Justice and Federal Bureau of Investigation. "Ted Bundy Multiagency Investigative Team Report 1992." *Santa Rosa Hitchhiker Murders*, n.d., p. 4, santarosahitchhikermurders.com. Accessed 3 July 2024.

CHAPTER 7. THE LAST MURDER

1. Tracy Smith. "Surviving Ted Bundy." *CBS News*, 4 June 2021, cbsnews.com. Accessed 3 July 2024.

2. Smith, "Surviving Ted Bundy."

3. J. Victor Africano. "Florida Trial Bundy: Theodore Robert Bundy, Appellant, vs. State of Florida, Appellee." *Scribd*, 15 Dec. 1982, p. 2, scribd.com. Accessed 3 July 2024.

4. "Bundy's Arrest Raises Fears for Girl's Fate." *Tampa Tribune*, 22 Feb. 1978, newspapers.com. Accessed 29 July 2024.

5. US Department of Justice and Federal Bureau of Investigation. "Ted Bundy Multiagency Investigative Team Report 1992." *Santa Rosa Hitchhiker Murders*, n.d., p. 41, santarosahitchhikermurders.com. Accessed 3 July 2024.

6. Africano, "Florida Trial Bundy," 3–4.

7. Jill Sederstrom. "Ted Bundy's Mark on His Face in His Florida Mugshot Has an Important Backstory." *Oxygen True Crime*, 31 Jan. 2020, oxygen.com. Accessed 3 July 2024.

8. Barbara Frye. "Suspect Is Recalled as a 'Nervous' Type." *Tampa Tribune*, 18 Feb. 1978, p. 10, newspapers.com. Accessed 3 July 2024.

9. Allie Norton. "Bundy's Last Stop." *WEAR News*, 13 Feb. 2018, weartv.com. Accessed 3 July 2024.

CHAPTER 8. THE KILLER ON TRIAL

1. Malcolm Lauredo. "Serial Killer Ted Bundy Found the Spotlight during His Miami Trial." *Miami New Times*, 4 Feb. 2019, miaminewtimes.com. Accessed 3 July 2024.

2. Ann Rule. *The Stranger Beside Me*. Gallery, 2018. 391.
3. Rule, *The Stranger Beside Me*, 414.
4. Wayne King. "Bundy Guilty of Murders of Two Florida Women." *New York Times*, 25 July 1979, nytimes.com. Accessed 3 July 2024.
5. "Bundy Sentenced to Die in Two Florida Slayings." *New York Times*, 1 Aug. 1979, nytimes.com. Accessed 3 July 2024.
6. Anna Moore. "Ted Bundy Bludgeoned and Almost Killed Me. I Resolved He Would Not Ruin My Life." *Guardian*, 27 Feb. 2024, theguardian.com. Accessed 3 July 2024.
7. Stephen G. Michaud and Hugh Aynesworth. *The Only Living Witness*. New American Library, 1989. 182.
8. Rule, *The Stranger Beside Me*, 439.

CHAPTER 9. CONFESSIONS AND EXECUTION

1. "Bundy v. Florida, 479 US 894 (1986)." *Justia*, 14 Oct. 1986, supreme.justia.com. Accessed 3 July 2024.
2. Kate Storey. "'My Name Is Ted Bundy. I've Never Spoken to Anybody about This.'" *Esquire*, 24 Jan. 2019, esquire.com. Accessed 16 July 2024.
3. Kevin M. Sullivan. *The Bundy Murders: A Comprehensive History*. McFarland, 2020. 60.
4. "Case File: The Search for Georgann Hawkins." *Killer in the Archives*, 27 May 2020, killerinthearchives.blog. Accessed 3 July 2024.
5. Rachel Floor. "Serial Killers Profiled at Mount." *Altoona Mirror*, 29 Apr. 2023, altoonamirror.com. Accessed 3 July 2024.
6. Dirk Johnson. "For Families, Killer's Death Eases Doubts but Not Pain." *New York Times*, 13 Feb. 1989, nytimes.com. Accessed 3 July 2024.
7. John Philip Jenkins. "Ted Bundy." *Britannica*, n.d., britannica.com. Accessed 29 July 2024.
8. Robert D. Keppel. *The Riverman*. Pocket, 1995. 141.
9. Jill Sederstrom. "Who Was the Victim That Ted Bundy Admitted Taking Back to His Home?" *Oxygen True Crime*, 19 Aug. 2019, oxygen.com. Accessed 3 July 2024.
10. Jenkins, "Ted Bundy."
11. "The Execution of Ted Bundy." *YouTube*, uploaded by Eyewitness News ABC7NYC, 31 Jan. 2020, youtube.com. Accessed 3 July 2024.
12. Maura Hohman. "Ted Bundy Survivor Responds to Controversy over Zac Efron's Portrayal of Serial Killer." *People*, 29 Jan. 2019, people.com. Accessed 3 July 2024.

INDEX

ABOUT THE AUTHOR

REBECCA MORRIS

Rebecca Morris is the author of several nonfiction books for students. She has degrees in English, international relations, and comparative humanities.